How Christ Changed Our Lives
Book 2

✝

Compiled by Wanda S. Mellette

"He gives strength to the weary
and increases the power of the weak."
Isaiah 40:29

How Christ Changed Our Lives
Book 2

ISBN: 978-1-60126-192-2

Cover Design:
Photo by Wanda Mellette, taken at
Mrs. Christian Ladis' Lawshe Run Cabin, PA.

Scripture quotations are from NIV;
Quotations may not be original with the author.

Printed by
Masthof Press
219 Mill Road
Morgantown, PA 19543-9516

In loving memory of
Floyd Ray Sensenig

My sister's father-in-law, my parents' good friend, and a man of God who never knew a stranger. God used Floyd's Homegoing to draw my daughter to salvation in Christ. It is in honor of his life and testimony that this book is dedicated. May God continue to bless his wife, Mary, their children and grandchildren.

• •

Floyd Sensenig & His Sons, Brian & Shawn
(My brother-in-law's favorite photo of his dad)

Special Thanks to my Father in Heaven,

my husband **Jerad**, our children, **Gabriel** and **Morgan**,

my parents **Larry & Sally Martin**,

and to my helpful editor,
Mrs. Erica Horst

Table of Contents

*Fictional name is used to protect author's identity

Dearest Reader:

Since "How Christ Changed Our Lives" came out in 2007, more people from my church - Christian Fellowship Church (CFC) - and people I know through my alma mater - Lancaster Christian School (LCS) - agreed to be a part of this sequel. Some individuals gave me their testimonies as far back as early 2008 while others gave theirs to me just a week before and one just 2 days before I was scheduled to go to the printing press! But each testimony, each story, each quote and each Bible verse contained in this book, I trust, will bring glory to God and will refresh your spirit.

Originally, I wanted this sequel to be published in June, so that people could include this book as a "Summer Read", but my plans aren't always aligned with God's plans. In late May of 2009, I found myself doubled-over in excruciating pain. My husband, Jerad, drove me to the hospital where I ended up passed out in the Emergency Room. I had many tests – ultrasounds & blood work – but, the doctors were still having trouble finding out what was wrong. One doctor came back to me and Jerad saying it was either a very large cyst or it was colon cancer. For someone with OCD (Obsessive Compulsive Disorder), this normally would have really freaked me out, but even in that moment of uncertainty, I felt God's peace sustaining me.

I was in so much pain. Having already experienced two Cesarean sections, I quickly realized how "easy" and "painless" they were compared to what I was feeling on that hospital gurney. Imagine thinking childbirth was easier than what I was going through! After a CT-Scan was conducted, they determined that I had a rip or a tear in my rectus muscle (Note: the rectus muscle is located in your abdominal region). Apparently, six days prior to this agonizing pain, I tore this muscle while exercising.

I was bleeding internally. Three pints of blood were now held up in some sheath in my abdomen. I spent four days in the hospital doped up on morphine. That first night in the hospital, I started noticing a lot of swelling in my belly. The doctor explained to me later that the swelling wouldn't go away until Labor Day. Groan. I swelled to the point that I now look like I'm pregnant! The doctor's orders were "No exercising for 6 months, no driving for 4 weeks and to resume 'nothingness' for 6 weeks." What a start to my summer vacation!

The second day home from the hospital, I received a phone call from my children's school, LCS. I was offered the part-time Middle School English teaching position! Now my "nothingness" wasn't quite so purposeless. God provided and continues to provide ways for me to feel productive, even as I "take it easy."

These days I walk around looking pregnant fashioning new "moo-moo" dresses. But things could always be worse. I have seen the goodness of God's people as individuals at CFC and at LCS have sacrificed their time and energy to prepare meals for my family, write encouraging notes & cards, and even provide me with a wheelchair early in my recovery so I could "stroll" the boardwalk on vacation. My family has also showered me with compassion as they bought me those attractive "moo-moo" dresses, loose-fitting clothes, groceries, cleaned my house, drove me wherever I needed to go and picked up my slack wherever and whenever possible.

In July, our new teaching pastor, Dr. Doug Bozung, shared a message entitled, "The Necessity of the Ministry of Every Believer". He used a visual illustration that touched me to the core. He held up each of his golf clubs and explained what each one of them are used for. One club allows the golfer to hit a ball 300 yards, another club just a few inches. But each club - when used to hit the ball - counts for just one stroke. Each golf club is important, each has its own purpose. Likewise, all people in the Body of Christ are vital – all have their own purpose – and all are necessary to accomplish the "game" of life. Had I not experienced this rare irritation of pain and discomfort, I would not have been blessed by the thoughtful care of so many wonderful saints. I was physically unable to do many things and if it hadn't been for God's people, I wouldn't have the recovery I'm having.

I'm learning the joy of my trial. "Consider it pure joy, my brothers, whenever you face trials of many kinds, because you know that the testing of your faith develops perseverance. Perseverance must finish its work so that you may be mature and complete, not lacking anything." James 1:2-4

I'm also learning that I don't know what others may be going through and therefore, I should not judge them. What must my neighbors be thinking when they see me pointing with my toes telling my children that they need to pull this or that weed and then to put it in the trash can? Why can't she do it herself? Since bending over is of utmost irritation, I can't help Gabriel & Morgan with any of the gardening. I am learning so many new things during this period of recuperation. God is still in the process of molding me and using me in ways as a result of this episode. I'm forced to use gifts and talents that I may have been neglecting before. I thank God for His working in my life in this way.

My prayer is that you will find time to sneak away and read each transforming story in this book. I pray that you'll be refreshed and motivated to do something for someone else and you'll become more passionate about your relationship with Christ. And if you don't have a relationship with Christ, I pray you'll start one.

There are many people to thank for the production of this book – my Heavenly Father who gives me purpose and who actively pursues a love relationship with me, my husband and best friend Jerad, my children Gabriel & Morgan, my parents, sisters, friends, and those individuals who gave their stories for this book. Thank you all!

Lastly, I want to thank dear sweet Erica Horst who agreed to help edit these testimonies. Thank you Erica for being willing to read countless pages and for giving me encouragement and feedback along the way!

To God be the Glory,
Wanda S. Mellette
July 2009

Chapter One:

I May Only Be 5, But I Know What I'm Doing

By Morgan Mellette (Age 5) & Mommy
(Wanda Mellette)

*"Don't let anyone look down on you because you are young,
but set an example for the believers in speech,
in life, in love, in faith and in purity."*
1 Timothy 4:12

When I turned 4 years old, I looked like this…

One month later, I looked like this…

See My Missing Front Teeth?

What happened? I had an unfortunate accident with a teeter-totter at the park. After it was all said and done, I had emergency oral surgery to remove my 3 front teeth! I look forward to turning 7 because that's when the dentist said I'll have my teeth back. I can't wait!

Two months after my teeter-totter accident on September 11, 2008, I made a decision that changed my life – let me explain...

On the way home from one of my mommy's Bible studies and after visits to my Aunt Lisa's and Aunt Jodi's, I out-of-the-blue said,

> "*Mom, I REALLY miss Pop-Pop Floyd!* (My Aunt Jodi's father-in-law, Floyd Sensenig, who died in a well-drilling accident 3 days after Christmas in 2007.) *I want to see him.*"

This sparked a whole conversation about trusting Christ as Savior, asking Him to forgive us from our sins, etc. After talking a lot about the cross and how Jesus is alive in Heaven...I prayed,

> "*God, I'm sorry for the bad things. Will you forgive me?* (Pause) *Thank you! Amen!*"

Mommy chatted about how important it is to tell others about Christ and how the Holy Spirit is living inside me now to help me know the good and godly things to say and do. Then, I "told" MeMa (Mommy's Mom) on the phone. Okay, I was really too shy to talk, so my mom just asked me questions and I excitedly answered! When we were almost home, I said,

> "*I need to make a phone call.*" I was pretending to have a phone in my hand as I "called" Pop-Pop Floyd.
> "*Pop-Pop Floyd, Hi. I'm going to get to see you. Do you want to come to my house?*"

It was a very sad time when our friend, Pop-Pop Floyd went Home to Heaven. The last time we were with him, we were celebrating my cousin Jeremy's birthday, and then 3 days after Christmas, he died. He left behind his wife - MeMa Mary, his children, his grandchildren, and even his own parents! But, like Mommy and Daddy say, "*God used Pop-Pop Floyd's death to bring me to Himself.*"

About 30 years before Pop-Pop Floyd died in a well-drilling accident, he lost his leg in a well-drilling accident. Even though he had a "fake leg", Pop-Pop Floyd would make everyone giggle when he'd walk on his hands at the beach! So, in honor of Pop-Pop Floyd, my mommy wrote a very special verse to the song "Jesus Loves Me" that me and my cousins (and my cousins' cousins) sang at his funeral.

> *"Jesus loves me even though*
> *Pop-Pop Floyd to Heaven go.*
> *He has 2 legs which to stand,*
> *No more walking on his hands."*

I'm still learning, but I know – without a doubt – that I'm God's child now and I know the Holy Spirit is living in my heart.

It's not always easy being a Christian. God allows us to go through challenging times that will, hopefully make us stronger, but will always bring Him glory. One tough thing I went through in January of 2009 was when I, once again, was the victim of an unfortunate accident. I got knocked over in the snow and my collarbone was fractured. I had to wear an uncomfortable brace for 6 whole weeks. It wasn't easy, but God helped me through it.

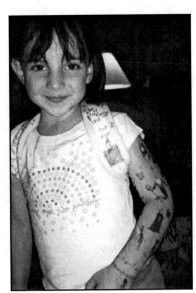

The fake tattoos on my arm helped my preschool friends know which arm to stay away from

My big brother, Gabriel, asked Jesus into his heart years before I did. He loves to read his Bible, pray and really wants to do things that honor God. Gabriel helps me grow in my relationship with God. We watched a cartoon about the martyred missionary Jim Elliot. In the movie, Jim baptized people who knew Jesus personally as their Savior. After seeing that, Gabriel said that he wants to get baptized so that others will know that he is a Christian. Some people may think that Gabriel is too young to get baptized because he's only 7 years old. And some people may think I'm too young to know what I did when I asked Jesus to forgive me from my sins and that the Holy Spirit lives inside of me, but I know what I did and I'm so glad I did it. In the Bible, the Apostle Paul said, "*Don't let anyone look down on you because you are young, but set an example for the believers in speech, in life, in love, in faith and in purity.*"

Chapter Two:

My World Came Crashing Down
By Amy Wentling

"Now listen, you who say, 'Today or tomorrow we will go to this or that city, spend a year there, carry on business and make money.' Why, you do not even know what will happen tomorrow. What is your life? You are a mist that appears for a little while and then vanishes. Instead, you ought to say, 'If it is the Lord's will, we will live and do this or that.'"
James 4:13-15

I grew up in a Christian family with two older brothers, Brian and Shawn. We were a typical family of five. My dad, Floyd Sensenig, worked hard with his family business and my mom, Mary, helped him in the office. Mom and Dad put a lot of time into the business but they always made time for us. We grew up at Christian Fellowship Church (CFC). We went to church on Sundays and Wednesday nights - sometimes more - when Dad was a deacon and Mom worked on the kitchen committee. We often stayed late waiting for Dad to finish fixing something at the church.

At the age of eight, I accepted Christ into my heart at Greenview Bible Camp, which happens to be right behind our house. I learned about Christ and how He died for my sins and how much He wanted to be a part of my life. I knew what I prayed was real, but I repeatedly asked God if I would someday be with Him in Heaven.

I was a typical kid growing up. Our family was pretty active. We went snow skiing and snowmobiling in the winter and water skiing, camping, four-wheeling, and motorcycling in the summer. We made many memories as a family.

During my high school days, friends were very important to me. My social life was my top priority. I wasn't fond of school much, so I always looked forward to the weekends when I could hang out with friends. Slowly, I went through some spiritual highs and lows. I was all about God, but then I would put Him aside. I couldn't imagine giving up the life I was living.

Senior year came and I had no direction for my life. Staying at home and working for the family business sounded like a good plan to me, but that was my plan. Little did I know what God's plan was for me. I took a trip to Word of Life Bible Institute for the weekend with some girls. I had no intention of going there for after high school. Besides, I wasn't living for the Lord. But while there, we sat in a few classes and I could feel the Lord tugging at my heart. I knew He wanted me there but I wanted no part of His plans. Needless to say, the Lord is more powerful than we are and I made a very quick decision to attend the Bible Institute.

By the end of the one-year of concentrated Bible at Word of Life Bible Institute, my heart did change and God showed me His presence was real. Returning home, I thought life would be easy, since I had been faithful to the Lord for the past year. In the summer of that year, I got connected with some old friends. We went out one night and returning home, we came upon a DUI (Driving Under the Influence) checkpoint. I knew it wasn't going to be good because I had been drinking. That night I got arrested for DUI. I remember feeling scared and in shock. I was questioning God - *Where was He that night, Why was God letting this happen?*

Looking back, I remember asking the Lord every day to draw me closer to Him - this wasn't what I had in mind. From that point on, I proceeded with a career as a hairstylist. I met my husband, Adam Wentling, and we got married in 2005.

Amy & Adam

On December 28, 2007, my world came to a stop. I remember I had off work that day because of the Christmas holiday. It was cloudy and the sky was very blue - to the point where it looked like it could rain. Around 3:00 in the afternoon, I got a panicked call from my mom telling me there's been an accident with my dad, but that he still had a pulse. On the way to Hershey Medical Center, we were still hopeful he was alive. We had learned that a well-drilling rod had struck him on the back of the head. People who knew my dad knew he had lost a leg in a well-drilling accident when my mom was pregnant with me. So, I thought since he made it through the first accident, he'd make it through this one. Finally arriving at the hospital, we saw Pastor Fred Raupp from a distance in another room. We couldn't see whom he was talking to, but keeping my hopes up, I thought he had been talking to dad who was probably lying there in his hospital bed. When they called us into the room, I could see the sadness on the lady's face. In my mind I was still pleading with the Lord that he would be okay. I never pleaded with the Lord so much as I did on that day. *Lord, not my dad. He's everything to me! Someone please give us an answer!* My mom kept asking, "*Is he dead?*" I didn't want to know - I just knew my world was crashing down. Pastor Fred finally answered, "*He's Home now. He's with his Father.*"

When someone dies they say you go through every emotion. I was very angry with the Lord that night, to the point I could have picked up a table and thrown it across the room. But then complete sadness came over me. I remember watching the rain coming down and feeling like all hope was gone. *Why, Lord, Why?* As days went on, friends and family showed support. I realized at his funeral he had touched so many lives. It was evident the Lord had used him to touch others. Only after his funeral did I realize that God was saying, "*He's with me now and he has peace.*"

"And there the weary are at Rest." Job 3:17b

"And I declared that the dead who had already died, are
happier than the living who are still alive."
Ecclesiastes 4:2

I believe now the Lord was preparing me for my dad's death. Dad was on my mind many nights as I was driving home from work. I always saw my dad as the center of our family. He worked so hard, but nothing would stand in his way of *living life*. He made sure everyone had a good time or he was going to see to it that you did! It was evident that he enjoyed life to the fullest. Dad was always someone I wanted to be like and who I couldn't imagine life without. Soon, those thoughts were interrupted with "*What if he would die?*" Those words were very chilling to me and I tuned them out of my mind. Little did I know that God was preparing me. I remember the last words out of my dad's mouth on Christmas Day - which he often said - "*I love you.*" I will always cherish that memory.

I miss my dad very much. There hasn't been a day yet where I haven't thought of him and wondered what his is doing up there in Heaven. I can't even image what Heaven must be like or what he is seeing and experiencing. I often wish I could take a peek, but then I would be begging to go there myself! It comforts me to know that Dad is at peace and someday will show me around Heaven. I can't wait for that day.

Eleven months after he passed, the Lord took his mother home to be with him in Heaven. I would have loved to see that reunion. Heaven has become more real to me through this experience. The words "*We are just passing through*" also have new meaning to me.

Amy, Her Mom & Baby Seth – December 2008

I still argue with the Lord sometimes, especially when I see my son (he was born the September after Dad died) playing with his truck and he looks up to give me a great big smile that reminds me of a smile Dad would have given me. I know I am still in the healing process and I need to give it time. I also I know I can't do it without the Lord.

Amy, Adam & Seth - Easter 2009

Chapter Three:
Confirmed Catholic
By Adam Wentling

*"For all have sinned and fall short of the glory of God,
and are justified freely by His grace through the redemption
that came by Christ Jesus."*
Romans 3:23, 24

I grew up in a Catholic home. My mom would take my sister and me to church every Sunday. My dad would normally only go to church on Christmas, Easter and a few other "important" Sundays. As most Catholic children do, I attended Sunday School classes to learn and to achieve the sacraments that are a part of the Catholic faith.

Just before my eighth grade year of school my parents got separated. My mom moved out, and my sister went with her. I decided to continue living with my dad in an attempt to keep my life as normal as possible. During that eighth grade year of school, my mom would still come to pick me up and take me to church every Sunday. It was my last year of Sunday school and then I would receive the sacrament of Confirmation, officially becoming part of the Catholic Church. Once I completed that, I stopped going to church.

The next few years are what I consider to be typical of that of a high school kid in America. I played one sport each season, hung out and played video games with my friends on weekends, and labored through the grueling school days at Garden Spot High School.

About mid-way through my sophomore year, my friends and I started to experiment with some of the more carnal things of this world. I began to drink alcohol and do drugs on a regular basis. Alcohol was more of a weekend thing and was harder to get a hold of. Drugs are much more readily available to a sixteen-year-old. This type of lifestyle continued on into my senior of high school.

Some Christians from school had been brought into my life. Though at the time I had no intentions of changing the way I was living, I had heard that the Christian Fellowship Church youth group was going on a ski trip. It was a weekend trip for a really good price, and since I did have quite a few friends in the youth group, I decided to sign up.

The day of the ski trip, we were to meet at the church right after school. Since I had not yet packed, I took it upon myself to write a note to leave school early that day. I cut out around lunchtime and went home. Once home, I decided to get high before starting to pack, figuring that I would be back to normal by the bus ride. As packing commenced, I started to read down the checklist that had been sent out. *Skis, boots, poles?* Check. *Hat, gloves, goggles?* Check.

Sleeping bag, pillow, toothbrush? Check. *Bible?* Uh oh. No Bible. I started looking on the bookshelves at my house, but all I could find was a really old one that was falling apart. I couldn't take that; the other kids would make fun of it, I thought. So I decided to make a trip down to the local Christian bookstore and purchase one, stealing one had crossed my mind.

As expected, there was a keynote speaker lined up for that weekend. After the second session, the speaker challenged all the students to get into the bunks and just read the Bible for fifteen minutes or so. Feeling what I will call "convicted" for the first time in years, I obeyed and started reading. That moment was the beginning of a change in my life.

Over the next two weeks, I decided that I had to prove to myself that I could stop drinking and smoking, before I could proceed with "becoming a Christian." Then, on Saturday night January 29th, 2000, I accepted Jesus Christ as my Lord and Savior.

Amy & Adam Wentling

Chapter Four:

Jesus, I Love You

By Donna Booz

*"Because of the Lord's great love we are not consumed,
for His compassions never fail. They are new every morning;
great is Your faithfulness."*
Lamentations 3:22, 23

While sitting on my Grandmother's knee, she asked me what I wanted to be when I grew up. I said I wanted to be a mommy with a ranch full of boys. I was a shy, lonely little girl. At the age of 9, I was saved in the neighborhood "*Good News Club*." John 3:16 is my life verse.

> "*For God so loved the world that he gave*
> *His one and only Son, that whoever believes in Him*
> *shall not perish but have eternal life.*"

My mother dropped me off each Sunday at the neighbor's church and another little girl befriended me there. She was my only saved friend and lived quite a distance away from me, but we kept in touch all of our lives.

As I grew up, I had a very weak foundation in Christ. To compound that, I associated with the unsaved neighborhood kids. I did the things they did because I wanted to be accepted. I dated unsaved boys at school and went to the prom with one. He, Bob, was killed a few days later on his motorcycle. I was usually on the back of his motorcycle. My friend, Ernie, whom I also dated, was always special to me and he would tell others, "*There's just something special about Donna*." He took me to Bob's funeral. I didn't know that Ernie would die the next year and I would be attending his funeral. Years later as Wayne, my husband, and I were listening to a missionary speak; the missionary began telling a story about his cousin who had been saved and who had gone astray after the divorce of his parents. He also told how the Lord took his cousin's life early as he was drinking on his 21st birthday and had died in tragic car accident. I knew right away that the missionary was talking about my friend Ernie. I didn't know Ernie was a Christian and Ernie didn't know I was a Christian. I cried all day, thinking that Ernie and I could have been witnesses to all the kids we knew. *Why did God spare my life?*

I soon knew why. I was to be a mother – not a ranch full, but a mother to 3 boys and a girl.

I met Wayne, my true love, at Sun Oil Company in Center City, Philadelphia. I was behind him on the elevator and I said to myself, "*I want to marry him." After 3 years of dating on and off, my mother, who had been saved and was growing in God's Word, told me that as a Christian I should not be dating unsaved men. She gave me the Scripture verse, "*Be ye not unequally yoked together with an unbeliever.*" Through a series of events, Wayne was saved and we were married. I had the verse I Corinthians 13:8, "*Love never faileth*" engraved in Wayne's wedding band. We desired to have the Lord as the center of our marriage and hoped to send future children to Christian school.

I thought when our children entered this world that being a mom was the greatest thing in the entire world. I love my children and their little ones, as I am now a Grammy of 11!

Our family was very close and did everything together. As the kids began dating, it was so much fun to have their future mates around. Our first son, Brandon, was to marry a girl named Terry. He had led her to the Lord and gave Terry her first Bible. She loved being a Christian and came to every activity at church, many times bringing her 5-year-old niece with her. She often stayed overnight at our home and we felt she had become a daughter to us. Terry went to see Esther Palmateer, a beautiful pianist, to pick out her wedding music. When she came home she was so excited, "*Mom! Mom! Wait until you hear the songs I picked: 'Beulah Land' and 'The Song of Ruth!'*" I didn't realize at the moment that "*Beulah Land*" had the phrase that said, "*Only a few more days of labor and I'll take my heavenly flight.*" Three days later, while on their honeymoon, the Lord took home our 6'2", 230 lb. firstborn son and his precious wife in a fatal car accident. This was the perfect plan of God. There are no accidents with Him.

I prayed that the Lord would send someone to me and could help me understand the heartache I was experiencing. My prayer was answered. That little friend that met me at Sunday School and grew up with me called. I thought that she had read about Brandon and Terry in the newspaper. She had, but she also had lost her daughter that same week in another fatal car accident. We shared many tears and blessings in the weeks ahead. I could literally write a book about all the things that God had done for us throughout this time of sorrow.

"*His way is God's way, not yours or mine*" is a line in a song by the Brooklyn Tabernacle Choir. It's a song about Mary and Martha and their brother Lazarus who was sick, died, and was buried. Jesus was four days late to arrive at their home, but he brought Lazarus back to life. The song continues by saying, "*My God is Great, when He's four days late, He's still on time.*" God's way is perfect. He never makes a mistake.

First Corinthians 13:13 says, "*And now abideth faith, hope, charity, these three, but the greatest of these is charity.*" This was the verse on Brandon and Terry's wedding program – it also was engraved on the top of Brandon's casket. Psalms 116:15, which says, "*Precious in the sight of the Lord is the death of his saints*" was on Terry's casket. My life verse, John 3:16 was also Brandon's favorite verse and is on their headstone.

At the funeral, Wayne preached on "*The Love of Christ*". Our best friend's daughter was saved that day, and soon after, her husband and children were saved. I say to my friend, "*Jewel, it was worth it all because we'll all be together in heaven forever.*"

A friend who was like a sister to me went home to be with the Lord shortly before Christmas. Before her Homegoing, we shared many thoughts. She teased me about seeing Brandon and Terry before me. She also said I would be so jealous of her because she beat me to Heaven. We were so happy talking about that. She's there now and I picture her waiting on shore where she said she would be, with Brandon and Terry, her arms open, waiting to kiss me.

The last words I ever said to Brandon and Terry were, "*I love you.*" I'm so thankful for that, but God loves them more than I ever could. They're in perfect love. I was never angry with the Lord. I thank Him that my children and loved ones are with Him and that soon I'll be there too, never to be separated again. I have treasure in heaven. What a great reunion to look forward to as I continue to serve my Savior with joy.

The Brooklyn Tabernacle Choir sings this song:

> *Not because I've been so faithful,*
> *Not because I've been so good*
> *You've always been there for me*
> *To provide my every need*

You were there when I was lonely
You were there in all my pain
Guiding my footsteps
Shelter from the rain

And it was you that made my life complete
You are to me my everything and that is why I sing

Jesus, I love you, because you care,
I couldn't imagine if you weren't there.

You are the joy of my salvation
You are the peace in my storm
You're loving arms protect me
To shelter me from harm

You are Alpha and Omega
The beginning and the end
My strong tower, my dearest and best friend

And it was you that made my life complete
You are to me my everything and that is why I sing

("Jesus I Love You")

I John 4:10 says, "Herein is love, not that we loved God, but that He loved us and sent His Son."

Chapter Five:

God's Amazing Love
By Bea Neely

"If you can't sleep, don't count sheep,
talk to the Shepherd."
-Mrs. Claire Corfey

I opened my eyes on that cold January 13, 1946. It was my twelfth birthday. My parents were coming. I was so excited. I had asked for a Bible, as I had never owned one. I looked out the window of my room at the University of Michigan, and I began to cry tears of homesickness, loneliness, disappointment and fear. A blizzard was raging, and I knew that I would be spending my birthday by myself. My parents were at our home across the state on our farm south of Grand Rapids, and I was at the University hospital, waiting to have surgery that week. I knew that my parents couldn't make the three-hour drive in such a storm.

The tears continued to flow as I lay in bed and thought about my family and my little fox terrier, Midget. My dad was the fifth of ten children, born in a two-room log cabin on a portion of his grandfather's large farm. My mom was the second of three children. She grew up in the town of Hastings. Mom and Dad met at a Grange dance, and they were married soon after. They believed God existed, but they were too busy with their six children and recovering from the Great Depression to give any time to God.

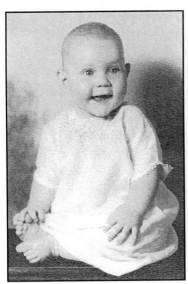

Bea at 7 months old.

Bea (2) and her sisters, Anges (4),
Joyce (6) and Lucena (7).

I was born during a blizzard. My dad had to go out to get the doctor because they didn't have a phone or a car. When the doctor arrived and delivered me, my mother and I were both near death. The doctor told my dad to name me so that he could fill out the birth certificate before filling out the death certificates. That is why I have my mother's name. At that point I had three sisters: Lucena-5, Joyce-4 and Agnes-2. Three years later Linda arrived. Three years after Linda, Fred was born. He did not lack attention! Obviously, mom and I both survived.

My childhood was probably as carefree and wonderful as most rural families at that time. I had lots of cousins who loved to come to our home. However, there was always lots of work to do, as is true with any farm. I was often sick with all the usual childhood diseases of the time. I had whooping cough, pneumonia several times, an appendectomy and Rheumatic Fever during which I had to stay in bed for three months - the standard treatment back then. It always took me a long time to recover and get my strength back. Books became my best friends, as I was confined to the house so often.

When I was eight or nine, a woman from the First Baptist Church asked my mother if she could take any of us to DVBS (Daily Vacation Bible School). Joyce, Agnes and I went. I heard stories that I had never heard before. I loved going to DVBS. The last day of the two-week school an invitation was given to accept Jesus Christ as one's personal Savior. I raised my hand. I didn't know John from Genesis. I didn't know theology or doctrine, but I knew in my heart that I was different. I had learned that Jesus was God's Son and that He loved me.

I had a wonderful Sunday School teacher, Edna Bechte. I believed in Scripture memorization. She even brought the class out to our house when I was too sick to attend.

When I was nearing eleven years old, it became evident that every time my left arm was bumped or hit, that I would get very sick. Pain in my upper left arm was becoming very acute. My parents took me to many different doctors. I was always diagnosed with the flu and given sulfa drugs. One specialist in Grand Rapids said that I just didn't want to go to school. My arm was shrinking and the pain was almost unbearable. I learned to sleep sitting up with my head on a pillow on my lap. My parents were at a point where they knew that they needed support. People from church would visit and pray with them. Our church family really showed Christ's love to my family.

In October 1945, we were sent to the University of Michigan hospital for tests and x-rays. A spot showed up on the x-ray. The doctors decided that it was Tuberculosis of the bone, and we were scheduled to be back at the hospital December 28 for surgery. The doctors would take a piece of bone from my thigh and replace the diseased bone in my arm.

As I lay on the bed waiting for no one, memories consumed me. My door opened and in walked someone who looked to me like an angel. She carried gifts wrapped in birthday paper. She was the wife of a resident and had come to the hospital to work that day. My sister, Lucena, was friends with her sister. Phone calls had been made, and she was my angel.

Surgery was scheduled for that week. When the surgeon cut into my arm, he closed the wound. A few days later, when my parents were able to travel across the state, they were given the news that I had terminal bone morrow cancer. The doctors had no record of anyone having survived that type of cancer. My parents were told as soon as I was able to travel that they should take me home. Today the word "cancer" strikes fear in the hearts of the ones getting the diagnosis. In 1946 it was an automatic death sentence.

After three weeks at home, my mom and dad couldn't stand seeing me suffer any longer, and they took me back to the hospital. They gave their permission for amputation, knowing that I probably wouldn't survive. When I went back to the hospital, I was put into a one-bed room. There were four-bed rooms and six-bed rooms, but the one-bed was reserved for children who were not expected to live. When we patients saw the drapes drawn in the one-bed rooms, we knew that one of our friends had died. There was no way to fight infections, so visitors (including parents) were kept outside the rooms and we had to converse through the long glass windows that separated the room from the hallway. I was put on two medications every four hours. One was morphine and the other was a new drug, penicillin, an experimental drug to fight cancer cells.

One morning, my room was filled up with doctors in white coats. One asked me if I knew what amputation meant. I said, "Yes." He said that they had to amputate my arm and that there was a probability that I wouldn't survive. My first reaction was "*Wow, I'll be free from pain.*" The second reaction was, "*Wow, I'm going to see Jesus before my friends.*" Later, as I thought about what the doctor had said, I decided that no one was going to tell me when I was going to die.

The night before my surgery, the First Baptist Church had an all-night prayer meeting for me and for my family. I was wheeled out of my room, and I saw Mom, Dad and Lucena sitting in the hallway giving blood. They couldn't touch me. The hall is where they had to wait—no waiting rooms back then. Dr. Harris did an arm, shoulder, collarbone and shoulder blade amputation. My dad was broken. During the surgery, he dropped to his knees in the hospital hallway and cried out to God. My strong daddy who could fix anything couldn't fix his little girl.

When I came out of the ether, my mother was sitting by my bed. I wanted to ask her if they took off my arm, because my arm still felt attached. I could see the bandages, and I didn't want to upset Mom. My mother found a small room near the hospital and worked in the hospital kitchen so that she could be near me. That put a lot of responsibility on my older sisters, but I never heard them complain. A hospital teacher kept me up to date with my schoolwork and reading. I was kept in the hospital for two more months. When told that I could go home, I was taken - cold turkey - off the morphine and the penicillin.

Right after I came home from the University of Michigan, Daddy took me to the Veterans Affairs Hospital in Battle Creek. I saw bed after bed and row after row of World War 2 veterans. We went outside and Daddy said to me, "*It is up to you how you want to live.*"

This was early 1946. There was no such thing as emotional, physical, chemotherapy or occupational therapy. There was radiation, which I had for months, but it was the old type of radiation, which left my lungs very scarred. My parents were advised to put me into an institution. When they declined, the advice was not to treat me any differently than their other children. My parents always told me that I could do whatever my sisters did as long as I figured out how to do it. One time I asked my dad to tie my shoes. He told me to figure it out for myself, and he left the room. I was crushed, but I did figure out how to tie them. Years later, my mother told me that when Daddy left the room that he cried like a baby.

The first Sunday after I got back home, my parents, Joyce, Agnes, Linda and Freddy, in daddy's arms, and I went forward at the end of the service as a show of our family's newfound faith in Jesus Christ. A month later, at our baptismal service, I gave as my Bible verse John 3:17, *"For God sent not His Son into the world to condemn the world, but that the world through Him might be saved."*

That first summer after I came home from the hospital, we went to Gun Lake. My sisters headed for the lake. As I sat on the blanket, my dad looked at me and told me I could sit on the blanket and have people feel sorry for me, or I could get into the water and relearn how to swim. Daddy never left my side, and I was swimming again by the time we left for home

We were making many trips to the hospital for radiation treatments. I would get sick each time. Cancer patients were treated like Aids patients were in the 80's. People didn't know where cancer came from or if it could be caught by contact. My last visit to the hospital was a week before I was married on June 15, 1957. I was advised not to have children and not to get overly tired. I often laughed as I recalled those admonitions, as I had three babies in four years; I went to bed tired and got up tired.

Jack and I met our sophomore year at Bob Jones University. Jack was an only child, who fell in love with my big, noisy, fun and loving family.

We were like most young couples at that time. Struggling to save for a house, dealing with Jack being absent so much due to working on his Master's degree at Temple University, his Army Reserve responsibilities, and church activities.

I had to really trust the Lord. Homesickness was a constant struggle for me. Memorial weekend 1971 my precious sister, Joyce, was killed by a drunk driver, leaving five young sons at home with their father. Nine months later, Freddy had his spleen removed with a diagnosis of Hodgkin's disease and given six weeks to live. My dad called the GARB (General Association of Regular Baptists) pastors in the Grand Rapids area and asked them to set up prayer chains for my brother. Daddy asked that they pray that Freddy live long enough to see his three small children grown. God honored those prayers and Fred lived another 28 years, until God called him Home in June 1999.

On January 28, 1979, after battling bladder and prostate cancer, my dad had a heart attack and went to be with his Savior. My mother passed away in 1990 from complications from Alzheimer's disease. She remained sweet and compliant to the end.

In 1975 I was diagnosed with Essential Tremors - inherited through my dad's side of the family. These tremors can be mild or severe. I had the whole tremor works—head, hand, voice and even my insides. This proved to be more of a handicap to me, than figuring out how to do things with one arm. After several consultations with neurologists, I chose Dr. Goldman, head of neurology at Hahnemann University Hospital to do a Thalamotomy. My primary doctor was against the surgery because of its very real chance of complications such as stroke, paralysis, heart attack or death. There were people all over the country praying for me as I had the surgery on January 6, 2000. My handwriting and my voice are still affected.

In February of 1999, Jack and I went to Florida to see Al and Aimee Wilson. Aimee and I went to the pool for the exercise class, and we noticed an elderly woman watching me the whole time. The next time Aimee went to the pool, the woman asked Aimee questions about me. She realized that I had been at the University of Michigan when she worked there. She remembered my case because she had done the pathology report. When Aimee asked her why she had not spoken to me, she replied that she thought that my scar was from that period, but she just assumed that I had died.

I have lived a very full life and amputation hasn't slowed me down. I am a college graduate and a former teacher. I am a mother

Jack and Bea's wedding day, June 15, 1957.

and was able to change many diapers with just one hand. I was a very active mom at the schools my children attended. I've water-skied. I climbed a mile up Mount Hood in Oregon. And, in August of 2008, I went parasailing with my 16-year-old grandson!

I am thankful that God has allowed me to be the mother of three great kids and grandmother to five wonderful grandchildren. Every night after my children were asleep, I went to each bed and committed my child to the Lord. The greatest joy is that they all know and love the Lord. Philippians 4:13 has been my life verse, "*I can do all things through Christ, who strengthens me.*" I can do all that God wants me to do, through the strength that Christ will give to me. I can be the person God wants me to be, through the strength that Christ will give to me. I can bear all that God allows in my life, through Christ who will give me the strength. Over the years, many people have asked me how I can love a God who would let a child suffer so much. My answer has always been the same: How could I not love Him? He loved my family so much (part of that world Christ loved, died and rose from the grave for) that I feel honored that He chose me to be the vessel to bring them to Him. God's love never ceases to amaze me.

Jack and Bea and their children, 1964.

Chapter Six:

How CHRIST Changed OUR Lives
By Irvin & Janet Wenger

"Direct me in the path of your commands,
for there I find delight."
Psalm 119:35

One thing is for sure; Christ has definitely changed our lives! First of all, He saved us and gave us a whole new perspective on life and a real reason to live! But He also changed our lives in another big way. When first saved, we never would have imagined the life that God had already mapped out for us – no, never would we have imagined spending the major part of our lives as missionaries in Guatemala. Actually, Janet was planning for a nursing career, and Irv was anticipating becoming a high school math teacher. But God had other plans! Proverbs 19:21 is so true: *"Many are the plans in a man's heart, but it is the Lord's purpose that prevails."* (NIV)

Both of us grew up in Mennonite families in Lancaster County. Both accepted Christ as Savior while still young; Janet at age 13 and Irv at age 12, both at revival meetings in our respective churches. Admittedly, later on in our Christian lives we understood better the plan of salvation and the relationship between faith and works. Nevertheless, our saving faith from the very beginning was placed in Jesus Christ; a fuller understanding came later. We praise God for both!

As we grew in years, we learned integrity, industriousness, and responsiveness to God's leading as integral aspects of our lives. We both thank God for Christian families and the values we learned from them. These values would later have their influence in the decisions we made and in the direction our lives would take.

After both graduating from Lancaster Mennonite High School in Pennsylvania, Janet studied nursing and went on to work in the pediatrics section of a local hospital while Irvin went to college to study mathematics. We began dating about a year later and decided to get married during Irvin's junior year of college. Upon his graduation, we went to Honduras for a two-year voluntary service assignment with the Eastern Mennonite Board of Missions. Little did we know then that God would use this missions experience years later to draw us back to Central America.

During the eight years following our return to the States, Lisa, Lori and Cheryl were born. For more than a year of that time we managed the Guernsey Farm Restaurant across from Garden Spot High School. Later Janet took employment at a hospital in

Lancaster while Irv worked as a purchasing agent for Charles W. Duty and Son, Inc., a manufacturing company.

Charles Duty was a Bible teacher whom God used in special ways in Irv's life. The biggest doctrinal question that we had to grapple with was that of the security of the believer. The second was the dispensational interpretation and comprehension of Scripture and of God's working through the ages. God led in our lives to help us understand the biblical perspective on these two issues at the same time that He opened doors for us to change church membership to the newly founded IFCA church in New Holland, Christian Fellowship Church. During those years, both of us became increasingly involved in lay ministries at Christian Fellowship Church – Janet in the area of music and Irv in the area of teaching.

The year 1978 marked a turning point in our lives. Up until then we were a fairly normal family working secular jobs. However, God had special plans for us in missions and began to work in us in wonderful ways. It probably should be stated that at the time, those ways did not always appear to be so wonderful, even though later we saw them as such. Let us explain:

Seven years after leaving Honduras, Janet and Irv had the opportunity to return for a visit and vacation. While on the island of Roatan we discussed the possibility that perhaps some day the Lord might want us to return to Central America for missions work. However, after giving it some thought and discussion, we quickly brushed aside the idea, commenting that our girls were still too young and the timing would not be good for us. In fact, we discussed the fact that since our girls had been born to us while we were still in our twenties, after they would leave home we would likely have a number of good years left for possible ministry in Central America. End of discussion!

Well, not exactly! The first Sunday that we were back in the States after that trip, God used Pastor Mervin Horst to call us up short on our plans. Pastor Horst was teaching through the Gospel of Matthew in the Young Married Couples Sunday School Class. That particular Sunday morning we studied the passage of Matthew 8:19-22. At verse 21, Irv strongly sensed that the Holy Spirit was trying to tell him something special. "*And another of the disciples said* to Him, 'Lord, permit me first to go and bury my father. But Jesus said to him, 'Follow Me; and allow the dead to bury their own dead.'" (NAS). Pastor Horst explained that the disciple's father had not yet died. The disciple was merely stating that his family situation was not ideal at that time for following Jesus' call. Pastor Horst said that for our age group it would be like saying "wait until the children are grown and away from home." Well, how much clearer could God speak to us? Indeed, Irv was sure that God was not in agreement with our conclusion drawn while in Honduras.

Reflecting on how Christ changed our lives . . . well, He was definitely up to something here! Janet continued to have reservations about taking our three little girls, then ages 7, 5, and 1, to a third-world country to live and grow up. Irv entered into fervent and sustained prayer for a period of three weeks just asking God to make His will clear to us. God knows how to change hearts! After learning of a family that had lost a child under circumstances that appeared to relate to their willingness to serve the Lord, Janet commented to Irv that she understood that if we used our girls as an excuse for not going to the mission field, God could remove that obstacle. Janet then concluded, "I'd rather go with them than without them." That night, with both of us in tears, we told the Lord that we were willing to go anywhere that He wanted us to go and whenever He wanted. God's ears are really open when His children pray like that and mean it!

The next day Irv was at the typewriter writing a letter to CAM International (CAM for work in Central America because of its solid doctrinal position and extensive ministry in all Central America) explaining his background in accounting and purchasing, and sharing that he believed God had us at the crossroads regarding missions work. In God's perfect timing, He orchestrated having a job description form from CAM's Guatemala Field Director arrive at CAM's office in the same mail as Irv's letter! The position that Guatemala needed filled was that of Administrative Assistant to the Field Director. Guatemala wanted someone with experience in the areas of accounting and purchasing. The secretary opened the two pieces of mail and put the two in the same envelope, saying later that she knew God was at work in that situation!

CAM sent us a photocopy of the job description form from Guatemala. Reading that brought tears to Irv's eyes – he knew that God was at work in all that was happening. Janet, after reading the job description blurted out, "*This fits you like a glove. We can hardly say 'no' now, can we?*" Of course we couldn't; that was pretty obvious. We completed our formal process of application with CAM, attended CAM's three-week Candidate School in the fall, and were appointed missionaries in November 1978.

But then we ran into another problem! Although Lisa became excited about going to Guatemala and Cheryl was too young to know what was happening, our five-year-old Lori developed a fear of going to Guatemala because of Indians and earthquakes. Both Irv and Janet tried to reason with Lori regarding the true nature of those dangers. However, as you might well imagine, a little girl's fears are not easily calmed with logic or rational arguments. She was still scared and said that she would stay back in the States with Grandma while the rest of our family moved to Guatemala. Our quandary – how can we get Lori over her unreasonable fears of Indians and earthquakes? Once again we earnestly prayed about this disconcerting situation. And once again God intervened in remarkable ways!

Lori was at home with Janet when the house began to shake. Lori's eyes widened like saucers and she asked, "*What's that?*" Janet responded that she believed it was an earthquake. Local news reports later confirmed that not only was it an earthquake tremor, but also that the epicenter was located just a few miles from the Lancaster Airport. As we looked at the map included in the newspaper article, we realized that the epicenter was very close to our house! That evening when Irv came home from work, Lori greeted him at the door with "*Daddy, guess what! I'm not scared of earthquakes anymore!*" It was pretty clear to us what God's purpose was in that earthquake tremor. Okay, one down – and one to go.

A few weeks later, Lori's kindergarten class at school got to attend a school general assembly that featured an American Indian family. That exposure to Indians was sufficient to erase her fears of Indians. So that evening when Irv got home from work, Lori ran to the door to greet him with "*Daddy, guess what! Now I'm not scared of Indians anymore, and I'm ready to go to Guatemala!*" In answer to prayer,

God had accomplished what we had been unable to do. How do you like that for a new concept?

God subsequently worked out dozens of situations, not least of which was providing our financial support, to get us to Costa Rica in 1979 for our year of language studies. After our year of language studies in Costa Rica, we relocated to Guatemala where we both became instrumental in the planting of a new church in Guatemala City, Salem Church. We continue to be active in Salem Church, and over the years have also been involved in the planting of several daughter churches.

For twenty years, Janet has been teaching music at the Central American Theological Seminary in Guatemala City. Her vision gave birth more than fifteen years ago to SETECA's School of Sacred Music. Currently, she teaches music harmony and theory classes in a classroom setting, as well as giving group and individual piano lessons. Janet is Coordinator of the School of Sacred Music and continues to head up SETECA's Department of Music.

After serving in an administrative capacity throughout the 1980's, Irvin was asked to become the Guatemala Field Director of CAM Guatemala, a position he held for thirteen years until resigning for continuing studies in Texas. For the past fifteen years, he has also been on the faculty of the Central American Theological Seminary as a part-time professor, teaching Bible, theology, and missions courses.

Nearly ten years ago, Irv became one of the founding members of a new missions organization, Fraternity for the Advancement of Missions (FAM), an entity promoting cross-cultural missions from Latin America to more spiritually needy areas of the world. As treasurer and a member of the Executive Committee of FAM, Irv helps screen and orient missionary candidates in addition to handling the accounting for the FAM missions agency in Guatemala.

More recently, God opened the doors for us to become involved in bringing servant teams from Christian Fellowship Church to Guatemala to help with Intermissions conferences. We certainly had not seen that one coming! God led in unique ways to put us right in the middle of that ministry. These teams have been the means of increased contact with Christian Fellowship Church, especially with the younger generation with whom we had little interaction previously. Again, we continue to see how letting God have control of our lives yields such interesting and unexpected results.

Over the years, we have sensed - in very real ways - God's faithfulness. One of the principal ways was in regard to our girls. Initially, we hesitated to respond to God's call to missions because of our girls. But after turning them over to Him and no longer clinging to that excuse, God worked in wonderful ways not only in our lives but also, and especially, in the lives of our girls. From God's working in Lori's fears before leaving for the field on through His special provision for their studies and subsequent marriages, He has proven Himself completely faithful! He showed us so clearly that He can take care of our girls even better than we can.

Janet & Irv

We praise God for His work in the lives of our family. Our daughter, Lisa, her husband, Eric, and family are currently CAM missionary appointees raising their support to come to Guatemala to work at the Guatemala Bible Seminary in Chimaltenango (we can't wait!). Our daughter, Lori, her husband, Bryan, and their family are CAM missionaries working in church planting in Queretaro, Mexico. And lastly, our daughter, Cheryl, and her husband, Chris, are working in Pennsylvania and helping to support the rest of us. All three love the Lord and want to serve Him where He has placed them. Praise the Lord!

We have been asked, "*What has been the biggest sacrifice for you when going to the mission field?*" For us, undoubtedly the greatest sacrifice has been separation – the physical distance from family. In the early years, we seldom got to see our parents and siblings, and the girls their grandparents, uncles and aunts. Then, with the girls' boarding school later, separation took the form of taking our girls from our home prematurely. More recently, we feel the separation from our grandchildren! We really would like to be closer and to be able to spend more time with them, but cannot. So separation from family ranks high on - in fact, tops - the list of sacrifices. Nevertheless, God has given us some very close friends (especially students from other countries) who have become almost like family, even calling us "*Mom and Dad.*" So there's been some give and take even in family.

Over the years, we have encountered a number of trials and difficult situations. Whether suffering physical illness with months in bed (Irv's hepatitis), facing dangers from guerilla presence in our travels, or living in the midst of street gang activity (current situation in Guatemala City), we have found that trusting our Lord fully is not always easy. We are human, and it can be tough. A wall hanging motto that we received for a wedding gift and still have hanging in our bedroom states: "*Never be afraid to entrust an unknown future to a known God.*" In many ways, this has become the motto and challenge for our lives as we face the future. Reflecting on God's faithfulness in the past gives us even greater confidence in His faithfulness – both for living in the present and for looking to what lies ahead.

Let us add a word here about how God used Christian Fellowship Church in our lives. First of all, after becoming members of the Church, we both grew in Bible knowledge, understanding, and appreciation under Pastor Irvin Martin's clear dispensational teaching ministry. Of course, that spiritual foundation has been key to our missions career and continues to serve us well. Secondly, Christian Fellowship Church has stood by us so faithfully throughout these past 30 years, partnering with us in prayer, financial support, and ministry teams. We sense this partnership not only with the Church as a whole, but also with many of its members individually. How we thank God for CFC!

As we look back on our lives and on how God led us to Guatemala, and as we reflect on our response to His leading and on the fulfilling ministries that He has given us, we cannot help but see in our own experience how a loving God moves His children along one step at a time to accomplish His purposes in their lives. What promised to be a rather typical life in the USA, God transformed into an international pilgrimage! Our ministries have been multiplied to the ends of the earth as former SETECA students minister in 28 countries around the world. Praise God! He knows best. One of our favorite Bible passages is Proverbs 3:5-6. "*Trust in the Lord with all thine heart; and lean not unto thine own understanding. In all thy ways acknowledge him, and he shall direct thy paths*" (KJV). Now that's a challenge to live by!

Irv & Janet

Chapter Seven:

God Is Listening

By Heidi Witmer

"There are no problems, only opportunities!"
-Mrs. Yvonne Miller

I grew up in a Christian home. My parents dedicated me at Ridgeview Mennonite Church shortly after my birth. I owe a lot to my parents for their dedication to raising me in a Christian home and setting a Christian example for me. I accepted Jesus Christ as my personal Savior when I was young. I was at home with my parents when I asked the Lord to pour His grace and forgiveness into my heart. I chose to make my commitment to God public through baptism at the age of 13. I met my husband Steve during our sophomore year in high school, and we dated for 7 years before getting married at Ridgeview Mennonite Church on August 2, 1997. God has blessed us with two wonderful boys, Caiden, age 8 and Griffin, age 6.

Caiden & Griffin

Throughout my life, I have experienced God's hand of protection around me and my family. When I was four years old, my mother and her sisters were out for a day of shopping with my cousins, my sister and me. We were all traveling in a van and at that time, children were allowed quite a bit more freedom when traveling in a moving vehicle. I was making my way from the front of the van to the back. Apparently, we had a little potty in the back of the van, and I needed to go. While making my way from the front to the back, my coat snagged on the door latch and the door flew open. I fell out onto the two-lane highway at approximately 40 miles per hour. A driver following our van said that I looked like a rag doll as I rolled behind the van and tumbled into the ditch along the side of the road. Miraculously, I was not seriously injured. I sustained only some minor abrasions and a few bruises. *God's angels were watching out for me on that day.*

My early elementary education found me at Conestoga Christian School. I attended this school up until second grade, but I was having difficulty adjusting to the 1-hour school bus rides. At the beginning of my 3rd grade year, my parents transitioned me into the public school system at Brecknock Elementary School in the Eastern Lancaster County School District. My education in the public school system progressed well. In junior high school, I made some lifelong Christian friends that continue to offer me support and encouragement. I met Steve in 10th grade and we dated throughout high school and college, seven years total.

Unfortunately, it was during college that I was the farthest from God. I always enjoyed going to parties and drinking some of my favorite drinks when visiting Steve at Penn State. During those four years of my life, I was not putting God first. I was living to have fun and not thinking about setting an example as a Christian.

While growing up, throughout my teens, and early on in my marriage - before children, I remember thinking I did not have much to worry about. I had wonderful Christian friends, loving parents, a dear sister, and a wonderful best friend in Steve, who now plays a dual role as my best friend and husband. After graduating from Central Penn Business School (now Central Penn College) I worked one full-time job and one part-time job so I could pay off my college loans before Steve graduated. Steve and I were married three months after he graduated. Two years later, we were happily married and Steve had found a job in his field, working for an international pharmaceutical company. Soon after, we built our first home, and a year and a half after that; I was expecting our first child. There was so much happiness in life and so much excitement. After having our first child, Caiden, and seeing the wonderful blessing that God had given us, I started to feel more anxiety in my life. I had a baby to take care of now, and the enormous responsibility that I felt caused me to start to worry about my health. Whenever I would hear that someone had been diagnosed with some disease, I would want to know what his or her symptoms were. Then I would think to myself, *do I have any of those symptoms? Could I be sick with a serious disease?* I never really told anyone that I was worried, but I know at times, my close family and friends could tell that something was bothering me. My relationship with the Lord had not developed much beyond trying to be good, giving thanks at meals and saying a quick prayer before bed. I didn't spend time in daily devotionals because having a newborn baby kept me busy and I used the excuse that I couldn't find the time.

Twenty-one months later, God blessed Steve and me with another baby boy, Griffin. It was so nice to see another one of God's miracles, but this new addition gave me more to worry about. I wanted to be the best mother that I could be to both of my children.

Shortly before my pregnancy with Griffin we had started to attend Christian Fellowship Church. We reunited with some old friends and met many new ones. Soon after, I began attending Moments for Moms and had the opportunity to participate in a program called Apples of Gold. These programs were outreaches our church offered for young mothers. Each of the outreaches includes prayer partners, mentors and small groups. It was nice to share prayer requests with other young mothers and to pray together for each other. I also learned about making time in my schedule to have daily devotionals. I found that even though I still struggle with finding the time some days it is such a good feeling to spend time alone with God in His Word each day. I am very thankful for all of the mentors and prayer partners that I have had through both outreaches.

In December of 2006, one week before Christmas, I was experiencing a horrible headache. I remember watching a news broadcast reporting that it is was the time of year when many people suffer from headaches. With the added stress of getting ready for the Christmas holiday, I thought that I was probably just manifesting my stress in a headache. I was taking pain medicine around the clock. I went to a chiropractor but with no relief. I went back to my family doctor where I was prescribed narcotics for the pain. Through it all, the pain never went away. My family doctor decided that I should have an MRI. I am a bit claustrophobic, and I had never had an MRI before so I was scared, but I didn't have much time to think about it since I was to go immediately to have the procedure done. I asked the technician how long I would be in the tube and several other questions about what to expect with the MRI. I remember going into the MRI tube and shortly afterwards coming back out. I thought to myself that was the fastest 45 minutes ever and couldn't believe it was over. As I got up from the table, the technician asked me to come to the phone because she said my doctor wanted to speak with me. My doctor proceeded to tell me that I must be transported to the emergency room because I was having multiple infarctions (mini-strokes). At this point, I was very worried and scared and started telling the technician about my wonderful husband and two boys, how much I loved them, and that they needed me. I remember asking the technician if I was going to die. She held my hand and tried to keep me calm. I was admitted to the hospital for 3 days in the neuro-trauma unit where I underwent many tests. The tests all came back with no answers. The doctors thought that it could've been a side affect from the birth control pill that I was taking, but could not tell me for sure. This left me with many questions. *Why did this happen and why can't the doctors figure out what caused it to happen?*

I had many special visitors in the hospital, and I will never forget my visit with one of our pastors. He brought in a piece of paper with a Bible verse on it. It was Philippians 4:6-9:

> *"Do not be anxious about anything but in everything, by prayer and petition, with thanksgiving, present your requests to God. And the peace of God, which transcends all understanding, will guard your heart and mind in Christ Jesus. Finally, brothers, whatever is true, whatever is noble, whatever is right, whatever is pure, whatever is lovely, whatever is admirable – if anything is excellent or praiseworthy – think about such things."*

These words were exactly what I needed to hear. When I worry, I should give my worries to God and pray to Him. I am in His hands and He is in control. Laying in my hospital bed those three nights, I was worried and scared. I wondered if I would wake up in Heaven or in my hospital bed. Since the neurologists weren't sure what caused my strokes and disagreed about what kind of treatment I should have, I knew that I needed to pray and ask God to be by my side and help me through this time. I could also feel a calmness and peace in that bed because I knew that my family and friends were praying for me. My mom also wrote down some Bible verses on a postcard for me to read when I was worried and I thank her for those.

I feel that I am growing with Christ daily through prayer, and I hope to pass on to my children the importance of finding time to talk to God through prayer. I know that God can and will protect me, and God can and will protect everyone I care about. He can help me through difficult and challenging times. I know that in my busy life there is always time to pray and talk to God about whatever is on my heart. I keep copies of my favorite Bible verse, Philippians 4:6-9, in my purse so I can read it whenever I need to, and I can give a copy to anyone that I come in contact with that might need to hear God's Word.

I also keep a piece of paper in my daily planner that one of my mentors, Marty Smucker, gave to me. It has 31 biblical virtues to pray for your kids. I find that I can read these and pray quietly when I am waiting in the doctor's office, stuck in a traffic jam, or on a long car ride where I am the passenger. There are two small books that can also fit in my purse that I like to read, "*The Power of a Praying Parent*" and "*The Power Of A Praying Wife*", both by Stormie Omartian. These books have wonderful prayers that I pray for my sons and my husband every day. I don't think they actually know that I pray the prayers in these two books for them because I usually do this when they are at school and work, but I guess after they read this, they will know that I am doing that! My husband and our sons mean so much to me. I thank God for blessing me with a loving Christian husband and two wonderful boys. I was so happy when Caiden and Griffin asked Jesus into their hearts with Steve and me last year, and I pray that they too will have a love for God's Word.

There have been several scary times in my journey in life so far, and I am learning to not only pray to God when the times get tough, but to pray to Him in thanksgiving every day for all that He has given me. When the time came to send both of my boys off to school and watch them get on the bus, it was very scary too. I didn't feel like I was in control anymore, but I have learned to know that *God is in control*; I can talk to Him at anytime. In the mornings before the boys leave the house to go wait for the school bus, we hold hands and pray together. I always ask God to protect them and keep them healthy and to help them to do their best in school. I know that He is watching over them each day when I am not with them. As God says,

> *I do not have to be anxious about anything but in everything, by prayer and petition, with thanksgiving, present my requests to God. And the peace of God, which transcends all understanding, will guard my heart and mind in Christ Jesus. Finally, brothers, whatever is true, whatever is noble, whatever is right, whatever is pure, whatever is lovely, whatever is admirable – if anything is excellent or praiseworthy – think about such things (Philippians 4:6-9).*

Heidi, Steve, Caiden & Griffin Witmer

Chapter Eight:

He Still Loves Me

By Jodi Martin

"The days can be long, but the years are short!"
-Mrs. Linda Hershey

My name is Jodi Martin and I am 30 years old. I have been married for eight years and have been blessed with two children. My walk with the Lord has had many twists and turns, which have kept things very interesting. After all, it is those unexpected events that have helped shape me to be who I am today. The most prevalent lesson I have learned through my journey is that God is good and He is always faithful.

Although raised in a Christian home, I did not personally accept Christ as my Lord until around the time I was baptized, at the age of 11. I knew at that time what baptism signified, but I had a lot to learn in terms of trusting God. As I reflect on my walk since that time, there are several events that seem to epitomize God's faithfulness and protection in my life.

One of the first times I was aware that God was looking out for me and had a purpose for me was during the summer when I was 13 years old. I was enjoying a fun afternoon of boating with my family and my best friend. My friend and I were both in the water tubing, when a boater who was not paying attention suddenly hit us both, head on. My friend, having only been grazed by the vessel, was pulled out of the water within a few seconds and appeared to be okay. As my parents recall, after a few seconds of sheer panic they remember seeing me surface from behind the boat that had struck us. I was just lying there, very still. Then I let out a scream. My brother-in-law jumped in and pulled me out of the water.

The operator of the boat that had hit us called for emergency help and they were able to get me to land and into an ambulance. The doctors who were awaiting my arrival later informed us that they were expecting the worst, as they usually saw these kinds of accidents result in loss of limbs - or even worse - one's life. However, God decided to protect and spare me. As I left the hospital that day after being discharged with only minor cuts and bruises, everyone was amazed. It was one of those defining moments in my life, a time when I was absolutely helpless and God had proven Himself faithful. The doctors couldn't believe there was not one broken bone in my body. They explained to us later that when the hull (the body of the boat) hits a person, usually it shatters bones. There was absolutely no explanation other than God's goodness.

As my middle school and high school years came and went, the memory of that day faded. Isn't it odd how quickly we forget God's life lessons? As I graduated from high school and headed off to college, I was only somewhat changed by the events of that day on the water. The light of that lesson grew increasingly dim as the years wore on.

In college, I was reunited with an old friend from high school. It had been several years since I had seen him. After a few months of dating, we realized quickly that God had a plan, and it was for us to start our lives together as husband and wife. We were married the next year. I remember being so happy that my life was coming together just as I had planned since I was a little girl; I was married and couldn't wait to have children. It was all working out! I had no idea the journey that God had in store for me. Never had I asked God what His plan was, because I had always assumed it was in line with mine!

Husband and Wife

After six months of trying to conceive a baby with no success, I started getting nervous. The doctor told me to stop worrying; that it would happen in due time. A year later, we were back to see her again with the same disappointing results. Starting to question God's plan and now medically termed to have an infertility problem, we were referred to a fertility specialist. Disheartened at the failed attempts to conceive, we headed off to the specialist with a renewed hope that our luck would turn around.

I falsely made that year sound like it sailed by but that is not the case. It was filled with anger towards God, jealously of friends with babies and was a trigger point for major stress in our marriage. After several tests, the specialist had me start with oral hormonal medication. I was then switched to injectable hormones, followed by five expensive procedures - including surgery. During this time, I experienced an awakening of sorts in my spiritual life. Up until this time in my life, I had assumed that because I was a good person and treated others with respect and love, that that God would give me the desires of my heart. But I was mistaken. I soon learned, after hours, months and years of tears, yelling at God, name calling, doubting I even loved Him or He loved me. There was still no baby. My husband, the great man that he is, under an incredible amount of stress himself, did his best to encourage me, but I felt no one could understand the pain and loss I felt within my heart. No one, not even God.

Upon reflection, though, God was undoubtedly there and was moving people in my life to show His love to me. One example of this was the afternoon I was sitting in our empty nursery crying when the doorbell rang. I reluctantly answered the door and, to my surprise, it was a friend dropping by because she felt God moving her to my house to tell me three words..."I love you." As she said those words it was as if God were standing at my door telling me it didn't matter how angry I was at Him ...that He still loved me.

As time wore on, my husband and I started considering adoption. We had talked about it before, but finally after a lot of prayer, we were both moved on the same day to start the process. I remember, after having made that decision, that I finally started experiencing some freedom from the burden I had been carrying. My focus was turned from myself to what God may have in store for us. After six months of paperwork, interviews and counseling, we were approved for domestic adoption and were anxiously awaiting that special little person, whoever he was, to join our family. Approximately two weeks later, we got the phone call; we were going to be parents!

Words cannot explain the joy that filled our hearts. God had answered my prayers and although I had doubted, He had proven Himself faithful! Our son came home with us two weeks later.

I believe that God has a plan for all of us but we're often too busy planning life out ourselves, according to our ideals, to be able to see it. In my case, God decided to bump me off my tracks because I was not headed in the right direction according to His plan. I was forced to make a choice: I could have lived a life of bitterness toward Him or decided to turn my circumstances around by giving a listening ear to what He had planned. I chose the latter and God truly satisfied the needs of my heart.

As the story goes, eight weeks after bringing our first son home, we found out that I was pregnant after 3 ½ years of trying! I am reminded of the passage in Ecclesiastes 3:1: *"To everything there is a season and a time to every purpose under the heaven."* God is continuing to draw me close to Him and I am still very much a work in progress. However, I've learned through all of these twists and turns that God had a plan all along. Thank you for reading this and may God bless you all.

Jodi's Children

Chapter Nine:

Heal the Wound, But Leave the Scar

By Kim Anderson

*"Live a life of love, just as Christ loved us and gave
himself up for us as a fragrant offering
and sacrifice to God."*
Ephesians 5:2

"But thanks be to God who always leads us in triumphal procession in Christ and through us spreads everywhere the fragrance of the knowledge of him. For we are to God the aroma of Christ among those who are being saved and those who are perishing." 2 Corinthians 2:14-15

When you drive through the charming town of Hershey, Pennsylvania, what can you sniff in the air? Chocolate! We journey to Christmas Candylane in Hershey each year with our children. The kids say, *"Smell that chocolate, we're almost there!"* That warm aroma wafting through the brisk December evening air invites us to visit Chocolate World. But, as the tour demonstrates, refining the cocoa bean from the tree in South America to what we enjoy in a smooth, rich, Hershey chocolate bar is a long process.

We all have defining moments in our lives, those moments that change us forever, but more difficult to distinguish is the refining process in our lives. We're all a work in progress; long periods of time where God is slowly changing us into the person He wants us to be. I hope through my testimony that you will be encouraged in not only the defining moments in your life, but energized to live daily through this refining process!

I was born into a Christian family. My parents have attended Calvary Monument Bible Church (CMBC) since the 1960s. I have two brothers – Barry and Larry. My brothers were 18 and 19 years old when I was born. I was nearly 3 when my oldest brother was married so I don't really remember anything but "Barry and (his wife) Cindy." I remember Larry living at home (he got married when I was 7). One night he led me in the sinner's prayer (a prayer of repentance). I remember asking if I had to pray it out loud. I was probably about 5 years old. Pastor Reid baptized me at CMBC when I was 11. Since I was "the second family," I attended Lancaster Christian School—18 miles one way from my home. While driving alone to school one rainy October morning as a high school junior, my car hydroplaned and I hit a telephone pole. My injuries were severe. The pressure from the seatbelt caused many internal injuries: 2 cracked ribs, collapsed lungs, a bruised kidney, a bruised pancreas, and a ruptured spleen. My liver starburst into five pieces. (The liver is an organ that regenerates itself.) I had a head injury and lost my blood volume 3 times over, requiring 44 units of blood and platelets. I had a 50-50 chance of survival. For the next two weeks, I was in a drug-induced coma, and my life hung in the balance. Twice I developed infections that nearly took me. It seems unreal to describe these details to you; it's almost as if I am talking about someone else, because God healed me so completely! He heard the prayers of his people literally all around the world. My brother, Larry, has a lot of spiritual insight. He says that Satan tried to kill me, but God brought me back because of the prayers of His people.

09/15/2008

Wanda Mellette & Kim Anderson

I wouldn't say that God used my car accident to get my attention or as a wake-up call for me—I wasn't running from God. Actually, that school year, I had been meeting a classmate (Wanda Martin Mellette) 15 minutes early every morning to pray together for our fellow classmates. But through the accident, I learned that God is sovereign. No matter how much you think things are up to you, God is the One in control. You are not in control of your life, God is. He is the One who ultimately decides what happens! I carry scars on my body today as a reminder of God's mercy in my life. People have asked me about plastic surgery, but because God allowed me to recover so fully, I might forget completely if the scars were gone!

The Christian group, Point of Grace, wrote a song that explains perfectly why I want to keep my scars…

I used to wish that I could rewrite history
I used to dream that each mistake could be erased
Then I could just pretend
I never knew me back then

I used to pray that You would take this shame away
Hide all the evidence of who I've been
But it's the memory of
The place You brought me from
That keeps me on my knees
And even though I'm free

Heal the wound but leave the scar
A reminder of how merciful You are
I am broken, torn apart
Take the pieces of this heart
And heal the wound but leave the scar

I have not lived a life that boasts of anything
I don't take pride in what I bring
But I'll build an altar with
The rubble that You've found me in
And every stone will sing
Of what You can redeem

Heal the wound but leave the scar
A reminder of how merciful You are
I am broken, torn apart
Take the pieces of this heart
And heal the wound but leave the scar

Don't let me forget
Everything You've done for me
Don't let me forget
The beauty in the suffering

Heal the wound but leave the scar

A reminder of how merciful You are
I am broken, torn apart
Take the pieces of this heart
And heal the wound but leave the scar

Whenever I look into the mirror and see the ugly scars, I remember God is in control and He has a plan for my life! God has a special plan for each of you, too. I don't know what it is, maybe you don't either, but God does. Ask Him to show you! Let the scars in your life - and we all have them – (mine are just in obvious places) serve as reminders of God's faithfulness in your life. The scars are reminders that God is in control!

My car accident was a defining moment. Another painful defining moment, and a "turn-up-the-heat" experience in my life's refinement process was the July day I sat in the grass under the shade tree and told my boyfriend, Peter, that I was pregnant. Just days shy of my 19th birthday and the summer after my freshman year in college, my teenage pregnancy story rings similar to ones you've heard before. Yet it is different because unlike others who say "pregnant and alone," I was not alone. The Lord was with me. God had not deserted me, even though I had deliberately chosen to sin, to leave the path of His will for my life. My closest friend was with me, too. He, unlike those in so many other stories, did not leave me either. He married me that summer, abandoning his plans to finish college at Moody Bible Institute. He didn't have to stick with me—he could've gone on to fulfill his plans and dreams. But Peter said that together we had made a wrong choice and now together we had to do the right thing. Our lives were not a double standard—I did not lead a double life of "sex, drugs and drinking," but sexual sin with Peter was an ongoing battle. I was ashamed and embarrassed to say much. I felt like I should be stronger than to keep falling down. *What kind of testimony was I?* I did not understand about besetting sin and didn't know how to find freedom. Subsequently, after I was pregnant, confrontation was so painful. I later learned that I was still living in sin—the sin of pride. God convicted my heart and several years later, at a revival crusade through Life Action Ministries, I stood before my church congregation to admit my sin and praise God for His forgiveness. I firmly believe that I have received His full forgiveness, but I do realize that I am suffering life-long consequences. (Don't get me wrong, life is good--but that's because GOD is good!) I feel free to share all of that, because God has set me free—I don't need to hide in the darkness anymore. In fact, a teenager at work recently announced that she was expecting a baby, and when I talked freely about my own poor choices, she looked shocked, "*I can't believe you got pregnant, you're all Bible-y and stuff!*" I was able to say, "*Just because I'm all Bible-y, doesn't mean I'm not a sinner!*" It gave me the liberty to go on and share the plan of salvation with her! So exciting! I am so thankful that God has brought me from that place where I don't want anybody to know about my past sins because I can focus not on the sin, but on God's grace in my life! Praise Him!

Praise God for His forgiveness! God is in the restoration business; He can bring beauty and blessing from brokenness. Our beautiful blessing, Emily Jean, is now in her adolescent years!

Kim & Peter

The first year of our marriage was horrible. We both had so much to work through. Since our early years, we've learned a lot about this thing called marriage. It's something we work at daily. Some days it's easier than others. Maybe someone reading this is struggling in his or her marriage. God is for *your* marriage! I know it's not easy. This is counter-culture, but self-LESS-ness is key to your marriage. Our society says, "*He wronged you, get out of that mess. You have a right to be happy! Find someone else!*" I heard on a radio program at a very difficult time in my marriage, "*Don't focus on finding the right person, but on being the right person.*" If you are married, God wants you to stay that way. You are with the right person, now work on BEING that right person for your mate. "*Don't focus on finding the right person, but on being the right person.*" I promised on my wedding day to remain faithful until death. You can only be responsible for your own actions. Regardless of how your spouse treats you, you promised to love him or her! You may not even like him or her right now, much less love him or her. This is so simple that it may sound silly, but begin to pray every day that God will give you love for your spouse. Read 1 Corinthians 13 and substitute your name for the word love. Pray it in thinking about reference to your spouse. "*Kim is patient. Kim is kind.*" See what God does!

Proverbs 3:5 and 6 says, "*Trust in the Lord with all your heart and lean not on your own understanding, but in all your ways acknowledge him and he will direct your paths.*" God directed our path several different ways in the next years—more refinement.

In 2000, when Peter had his physical to renew his Commercial Drivers License (CDL), they said, "*How did you get a CDL in the first place? You can't drive a truck with your vision!*" We knew he had an uncorrectable eye condition in one eye since childhood, but it came as a shock that he shouldn't have ever been on the road with a CDL.

Needless to say, he lost his truck-driving job! We really had no idea what to do! Neither one of us has a college education. *Do we go back to school? Move across the country, somewhere cheaper? Do we look for something completely different?* After waiting nearly 8 months for a federal waiver from medical regulations (which was denied), God moved Peter to his current place of employment at BRT (formally known as Buck Run Transport Company) - not driving, but dispatching - right here in Parkesburg! Peter is still in the trucking and petroleum industries, the only two areas where he has experience. Only God could have done that! Also during that time of transition, Peter and I were able to serve on two mission teams – one to Mexico and one to Ukraine. We had another baby - our son, Tyler Jensen, and we built our first home. We learned a lot about God's timing and God's direction.

In 2004, I began attending an amazing Bible Study called *Bible Study Fellowship* when God began to work in my heart. *Bible Study Fellowship* (BSF) is an intensive Bible study - no coffee, no donuts, not much chitchat, and they even discourage use of study aids like commentaries and Bible dictionaries...it's literally just you and God (through the Bible)! I attended the class of about 200 women in Reading, Pennsylvania. That year's study was on the Life of Paul. I would strongly encourage any of you to attend a class if you ever get the chance! The second half of the year, I kept hearing over and over, "*What is God calling you to do?*" I heard an advertisement on the radio one morning on my 45-minute drive to BSF about a class offered by CEF (Child Evangelism Fellowship) called Teaching Children Effectively. At the time, I had a 2-year-old and a 7-year-old and I helped out at church in the children's program; I could use help in teaching children effectively! Peter agreed to take the 13-week class with me and we kept hearing other class members talk about "*After-School Clubs.*" That April, we went to a dessert social sponsored by CEF about *Bringing the Bible Back to Every Public School.* I caught the vision that night for sharing the gospel with children through the *After-School Good News Club!* I will never forget, Matt Staver, an attorney from the Liberty Council who explained how legislation in 2001 clarified that public schools could legally have Bible clubs on school property. He challenged each of us to be on the front lines in our own schools. He talked about how 12 spies were allowed to go into the Promised Land. *How many entered the Promised Land because of their faith and obedience?* Only two! I wanted to be like those two spies, to enter the Promised Land! I told my Moms In Touch Group (a prayer group) about it and we started praying for a club. My home group (a small group from church) started praying about it. I told a bunch of individuals—to get the word out! I was on our missions committee then and I shared it at a committee meeting, to get the church on board…what a huge mission field in our own backyard and we're allowed to go in and preach the gospel! By May I was convinced that God was calling me to start a club at Pequea Valley (my children's public school)! There were only a handful of clubs in Lancaster County then—and there are 80 elementary schools! Now, in 2009, there are more than 30 clubs! It seemed like an impossible calling, but when God calls, He equips. Peter and I had just taken the *Teaching Children Effectively* (TCE) course and we also had been asked to *organize and lead* a summer Vacation Bible School in Yaak, Montana.

The next January, I sat at my dining room table on the phone with our school's principal. After I hung up, I danced around the house with Emily because *"She said yes!"* With 7 leaders and 75 kids, the *After-School Good News Club* at Paradise Elementary began in February 2006! In those 6 weeks, about 20 children trusted Christ as their personal Savior. It had been nearly 10 months of prayers and much preparation—God preparing me (and others) so He could work in our lives and work through us and help others! There was a lot of work that went into starting up a club. Oh, and, I forgot to mention that I was 8 months pregnant! There were days when I wanted to sit home and put my feet up, not work on *Good News Club* (GNC) stuff, but God enabled me. At the end of my pregnancy, my prayer was—and many others were praying also - that I could finish the GNC semester before the baby came. I went into labor with Carly four days after the last club. God is good!

What is God calling you to do? What work does he have for you? Does it seem impossible? When God calls, He equips. CEF taught us that God uses <u>FAT</u> people—<u>F</u>aithful, <u>A</u>vailable, <u>T</u>eachable. Be obedient to him! Step out in faith to be that "FAT" person!

Right now I am trying to be obedient to God's call on my life as I witness to co-workers, as well as being a Christ-like wife and mother—boy is that a challenge!

My lifelong process of refinement wouldn't be complete without my sharing a recent defining moment of struggle. On May 4, 2007, my beloved father was diagnosed with Alzheimer's Disease. No one can really understand how dreadful this monster of a disease is until it is experienced firsthand. Watching someone I love very

Kim & Peter's Children

much become a stranger that bears only a physical resemblance to the person I once knew is almost beyond description. Dad is slipping away deeper and deeper into a place where no one can reach him. But what a precious reminder that he is never out of reach of the hands of the Almighty God! Recently, I was literally crying to God about how hard this is on my children—how it's not fair to them and how they don't understand. God brought a thought to my mind, "Yes, but think what kind of people this will make them." More refining! Sometimes I think, "God if you turn up the heat any more, there will be nothing left of me to refine! I'll be all burned up!" But God will not give us more than we are able to handle. With the Holy Spirit within us, we have all we need to bear our load!

Take a minute to reflect on your own life. My story is not more significant or special than yours. We all have our defining moments in this refinement process. What are you going to do with yours? Use your heartaches in life to make you better, not bitter. Think back to how God has carried you through some of your difficulties. And remember that God's got a great track record! He's been so faithful to you! Let me close with this verse, Philippians 1:6, *"Being confident of this, that he who began a good work in you, will carry it on to completion until the day of Christ Jesus."*

   "God, we praise you for your faithfulness! Thank you for walking with us through struggles. We have so much to be thankful for; make us grateful people! May we choose today to view our trials as opportunities to become more like your Son, Jesus Christ, for it's in His name we pray, Amen."

Chapter Ten:

Driven to Serve
By Grace Discavage

"God's work done in God's way will always have God's supply."
-Dr. Doug Bozung

"*That God chose me to be His child and serve Him, will never cease to amaze me.*" Many years ago, I saw this quote and wrote it in my Bible, to remind me, Who it is, I am privileged to serve and Who it is, I can call Abba/Daddy and Who calls me "friend". What amazing love!

I grew up in western Pennsylvania, living on a 100-acre farm. We were not farmers; we only raised enough crops for the family and for our animals. Our dad worked for the Pennsylvania Railroad. Our mother was a stay at home wife and mother. Our mother was dedicated to the family, and Proverbs 31 sums her up very well. When I hear the word "integrity", I think of my parents. Many lessons and values were taught and lived out in our home. I lived in a happy home where I felt loved, safe, and secure. I am number eight in a family of thirteen children. Growing up in a large family is a great experience. A love for God, country, family, music, humor, and reading were instilled in me by the example of my family. I enjoyed children and helping them to learn.

The Farm House

Having older siblings, I had good examples, and having younger siblings, hopefully, I was an example to them. I became an aunt at age 12 and always had nieces and nephews to care for. I was also blessed with a younger brother who was a Downs Syndrome child.

What a blessing he was! I enjoyed helping him. He and I shared much joy when he learned to do different things. Such excitement came when he learned to write his own name! He was the one person who shaped my life the most. He was a very wanted and loved child, and I thank God for giving him to our family! When he went to Heaven, and was made "perfect", he left a huge void in our family.

I always knew God was real and was the only One who could and would be my Redeemer. All I needed to do was acknowledge Him, confess my sins, and accept His love and forgiveness. I made this decision as a child during Bible School at our home. When I was about 17-years-old, I went forward during a Sunday evening service to dedicate my life to Him.

Since I had a Godly dad, it was easy to trust my Heavenly Father, and when I chose a future mate, I found one who had integrity and the gentle, caring spirit that my dad had. (*Dads, don't underestimate your role in your children's lives!*) After Jim and I got married, we moved from the area where we both were born and raised and moved to Delaware County, Pennsylvania, which we called home for 26 years. This was where our son was raised and educated. We were involved in the ministry at church; I taught Sunday School for the 2-4 year old children and Jim and I taught Junior Church during the morning service to the primary grades. I also served on the Ladies Fellowship Committee where we were involved with missions in many ways. Jim taught Sunday School to 4th-6th graders and adult classes, he served on the church board, and worked in the Boy's Christian Service Brigade program. My reason for stating these ministries is that while serving in these ministries, we matured in our faith and in learning of the Word. The teacher always grows in the Word when preparing lessons for the students.

It is important to know the gifts the Lord has blessed us with and use them for His Glory. As I write this, I thought about my gifts over the years in my walk with the Lord.

(1) We *must* reach our youth (Deuteronomy 6:7)
(2) Send, give, and encourage missionaries (Matthew 28:19)
(3) Uplift and encourage other believers
(4) Pray (1 John 5:14-15)

Prayer was always emphasized as a means for God to fulfill His plan. What a blessed thought ~ that God wants and desires to hear from me. God has proven Himself faithful, even though He does not need to. His faithfulness is very evident. Today, I see the prayers of my parents in the lives of 3 generations serving Him, on mission fields, in the pulpit, in medical ministry, as Christian schoolteachers, in music ministry, as elders, and serving in different ways in their local churches. I remember my dad and a few men sitting around our kitchen table discussing spiritual things, and one thing I remember them discussing is the verse in Revelations about everyone on earth seeing the 2 witnesses. They wondered how that could happen ~ but to our generation, it is no mystery, as we see live coverage everyday without being impressed. At that time, it was not a reality, but they believed it because God's Word said, it would happen ~ they just did not know how!

When Wanda asked me to write for this book, I asked "*Why Me?*" My life has been so secure, I have lived a pampered life, and wondered who would be touched by my testimony. Wanda sweetly reminded me that I, too, was saved from my sin and for His glory. It reminded me that I was just as guilty and sinful as what the world sees as the worst possible sinner. Jesus would have died only for me and for that, it humbled me to praise Him. Another church friend, Vivian Hertzler, suggested I write a praise I had shared with her, and I thought, "*Yes! Why not give Him the glory?*" Often, I pray and ask God for help and directions, only to take it back with "*what if*", but this was one time I gave it to Him and *never* took it back, because I *had* to rely on Him. I could not do it on my own.

Growing up, I had no interest in cars and never drove the tractors like my siblings. I was more comfortable guiding little ones, polishing furniture or cleaning floors, and so, I never learned to drive. While living in Delaware County, I could walk wherever I needed to go. But when we moved here to Lancaster County, everywhere I needed to go required driving, so I depended on my husband, Jim.

When Jim came down with a lengthy illness, I was at the mercy of others for everything we needed. Even though our son, daughter-in-law, people from church and neighbors were more than willing to take me wherever I needed to go, I did not always receive it very well, as I felt like a burden. I also felt hopeless. One Sunday morning, our son had picked me up for Sunday School and I never got to class as I talked to Larry and Tammy Martin and Meps Gardner. The impromptu trio encouraged me that I should learn to drive; I choked up as it frightened me. Meps told me she learned to drive in her later years. Larry and Tammy expressed that I could - and should - do it, but Larry (a policeman) requested that I never drive in his district, as he did not want to give me a ticket. He was so funny! I was not thinking in his terms that I could ever get a ticket, as I never expected to drive. The three of them were such an encouragement and I thought it was good advice, but it fell on "deaf" ears, as it was not possible that this fearful 59-year-old who never sat behind a steering wheel, could drive. We talked during the Sunday School hour, and then went into the sanctuary for the church service. That Sunday morning, the Adventure Club gave their wonderful presentation. Becky Myers always selected one child each time to do a verse and this week, our 5-year-old granddaughter, Cayla, was the one who was selected to recite the verse. The verse was Philippians 4:13 and it hit me, God was speaking to me, that I can do it through Him, if He willed it. I began to cry and said, "*Lord, if this is your will for me, I will try it.*" When I got home from church, I called Jim at the hospital and shared this with him. We came up with the idea to call the local school and ask them if the school had a teacher who gave private lessons. On Monday morning, I called and the person who took my call told me that the school's driving instructor did not give private lessons, but she knew of an older teacher who taught in the Downingtown School District and lived in New Holland. She gave private lessons and it sounded like a good fit. I knew that with God's leading we would be a good team. I called the teacher and she came to our home. She showed me the manual and explained what I needed to do. In talking, we realized we were both Christians and bonded right away. During each lesson she would pray with me, which was a real blessing. (Later, she taught driving instructions at the local Garden Spot High School.)

One day as our 2 granddaughters and I were having lunch, sitting at their little table and chairs, Cara, who was 2 ½-years-old, asked the blessing. She prayed for Grandma and said something about driving. She was so young, I was not exactly sure what she prayed but knew "Grandma" and "driving" was in her conversation with God. I sat there dumbfounded, as I had not told them what I was planning to do . . . *was this prompting from God?*

When Jim's health improved, he took me for my learner's permit and I passed the written test ~ *TO GOD BE THE GLORY!* We stopped at our son's home and told them what we planned to do. They were very supportive. I took 6 lessons, and asked for 2-3 more to gain more confidence. Before, going for my driving test, the teacher and Jim went over with me what to expect. On the day I went, I felt confident that I knew what I needed to do. But, no one told me I would be asked to turn on the car lights and turn signals before the officer giving me the driving test got in my car, and it threw me off. I went blank and I could not even remember how to turn the lights on, and then of all things, I turned the windshields wipers on. I felt so stupid and doomed as they swished across the dry windshield. (We laugh about it now). The Lord gave the officer the wisdom to give me a little time. He told me to relax and that he would be back in a minute. He walked away and I prayed. In a minute or two, he came back to a much calmer lady and then I knew what to do.

During this time, Jim was standing inside the center watching all this and said, "*Oh no! She failed before the officer even got in the car!*" But, Jim prayed for the officer and me. As we were driving, the officer asked me what made me finally decide to get my license and I told him, "*So I could be there for Jim.*" He said, "*You are a good wife.*" When we finished the test, he did not tell me if I passed or not and I was sure that I hadn't, but thanks to the Lord's goodness, *I passed!* The officer enjoyed teasing me by making me wait to know if I failed or passed. He told Jim what a caring wife he had and to encourage me to keep driving.

God placed people in my life at "*such a time as this*" to encourage me to obey and trust Him. These included Larry, Tammy, Meps, Becky, a lady at school, my driving instructor, the officer who gave me the test, and my family, (especially our granddaughters). I have never seen this miracle apart from God's Hand in it. Had I learned to drive at 16-years-old, I would have missed His blessing. I only had *Him* and to this day, I never start the car without praying and thanking the Lord for His goodness and His protection.

Shortly after I started driving, our granddaughter, Cayla, gave me a bookmark with Philippians 4:13 on it and it has been hanging from the mirror of my car from that day. It is now somewhat faded, but is a reminder to me of God's goodness. *Don't limit God!* When I started driving, I told Jim I wanted a Dodge Viper but instead, I got his '95 Ford Escort and he got a new car. The other day I reminded Jim that I never got the Viper, and now I am willing to lower my standards and accept a Saturn SKY, but the '95 Ford Escort and I are still a team. (Seriously, I am very happy with my Escort).

We were blessed in Delaware County with good sound teaching, and we grew spiritually. We completed studies at a Bible Institute and in doing His service, we grew to love, serve and obey Him. For many years, we had a home Bible study, some of us meeting for the first time at our first study; the group became family. It was such a blessing to see the different men lead the study, to see their growth in leadership, and then see the spiritual growth in each of us - many who began the studies as "babes" in Christ.

We have seen God use us where He has placed us. Twenty years ago we moved to this area. Since then, we had the joy of becoming grandparents. We both love being grandparents and thank God everyday for the blessing of having this privilege. I count it all joy to pray for my family and pray that our grand girls, as they mature, will honor Him with their lives. My prayer for my family has been that they will know Him and walk in Truth: 3 John verse 4, "*I have no greater joy than to hear that my children are walking in the truth.*" Recently, Jim retired and this is a new and wonderful adventure for us.

Remember: no matter what you or I may be going through, good times or difficult times, *God is near* and if He seems far away, remember the old saying, "Guess who moved?" If you are going through trials, they will help you grow spiritually and if you are experiencing joy and blessings, thank and praise Him. If your heart is right before Him, no matter your circumstances, all will be well. "*Keep the heart right, even though it is sorely wounded*" (or bursting with joy).

As I read the Bible, I am amazed at something new I did not see before; His Word is new everyday! A few of many truths and verses which bless me are: How the Bible starts out in Genesis 3:23-24 with such sad words as God sends Adam and Eve out of the garden (sin) but how it ends with joy in Revelations 22:4 where it states *"We shall see His face."* Habakkuk begins with a "sob" and ends with a "song" in 3:17-19. A few verses of what is required of us are in Ezra 8:22 and Micah 6:8, to live and walk with Him. In Philippians 3:10, we read that we must *know* Him and realize His work will be accomplished when His people pray, witness and obey. I also appreciate Romans 12:1-2, which says:

> *"Therefore, I urge you, brothers, in view of God's mercy, to offer your bodies as living sacrifices, holy and pleasing to God—this is your spiritual act of worship. Do not conform any longer to the pattern of this world, but be transformed by the renewing of your mind. Then you will be able to test and approve what God's will is—his good, pleasing and perfect will."*

And I love to claim like Job, in 19:25: *"I know that my Redeemer Lives."*

We really are light in the darkness and if we let our light shine, God will be honored. We were left here after we became believers to glorify Him....what am I doing to accomplish this and what are you, reader, doing to bring glory to Him? He - and He alone - is worthy of our praise. "The Lord's eyes are on His children, and our eyes should be on the Lord". Do I stumble and fall? Yes, daily! Do I give up? No. I know that at times, I am out of His will, but I am never out of His care. After we are saved, and we sin, do we lose our salvation? Never! (Hebrews 10) He died once for all our sins, past, present and future. He paid in full with His Blood and we are covered forever with His Blood. When I sin, I praise Him, confess my sins, and then strive to obey and please Him. I will continue to sin until He takes me Home or comes back, and may that be today. Even so, *"Lord Jesus, return now,"* is often part of my prayer.

Thank you for the privilege of sharing my thoughts and thank you, for taking the time to read this. As I give this to Wanda, it will be with prayer, that it may touch one life.

Chapter Eleven:
Answered Prayer
By Kaylee Glessner (Age 7)

*"You can't go wrong if your ambition is
to please the Lord."*
-Rev. Robert Shelley

My name is Kaylee Glessner. I am 7 years old and am in third grade at Lancaster Christian School. My favorite part of my school day is gym class. I have one older sister, one older brother and one younger brother.

Ben, Josh, Taylor & Kaylee

As my mom and I were coming home from the grocery store one day when I was four-years-old, I asked my mom, *"How do you become a Christian?"*

She said, *"You have to ask Jesus in your heart."*

"How do you ask Jesus in your heart?" My mom explained how to ask God for forgiveness through prayer. When we finally got home, I decided to ask God to forgive me and to come into my heart.

"Mom, how did He (the Holy Spirit) come into my heart? I didn't see Him come in there?"

"He's invisible, so you can't see Him."

"Oh, that's how it works!"

Since then, I continue to learn how to grow in my relationship with Him. I pray to Him often. It's really neat seeing God answer my prayers. During the summer of 2009, I almost wasn't able to go to

Greenview Bible Camp – a camp that spiritually challenges campers through Bible lessons, chapels, cabin devotions and scripture memorization. Activities at Greenview Bible Camp include crafts, archery, basketball, creek stomping, horseback riding, swimming, volleyball, go-karts and fishing. I really wanted to go but my mom didn't think we could afford it this year. I asked her if we could pray about it and she said, "Sure!" Even up to the day before day camp was to start, we weren't sure whether I could go, but God provided the money and I had an awesome week at camp!

My favorite Bible verse is John 3:16, "*For God so loved the world that He gave His one and only Son, that whoever believes in Him shall not perish but have eternal life.*"

Chapter Twelve:

Do I Have Value?

By Vicky Martin

*"But God demonstrates his own love for us in this:
While we were still sinners, Christ died for us."*
Romans 5:8

I am a transplant from Jackson, Michigan. I was raised on a small farm northeast of the city of Jackson. My family was not believers or churchgoers. Sunday was just another workday for our family. I was saved at a Child Evangelism Fellowship booth at the Jackson County Fair when I was about 8 years old. It was customary for all of the kids in our area to go to Vacation Bible School (VBS) every summer. Uncle Fran the Bible Man was a fantastic teacher and really made the Bible come alive. Growing up most of my knowledge of the Bible came from Uncle Fran during VBS when he taught us kids at school every month.

As a child, I knew I was saved but that was all I knew. When I was in Junior High, my Girl Scout leader invited me to her church. My mom would drop me off at church and pick me up when the service was over. It was a very small church but it was just the place for me to learn about the Lord. The church would sing many hymns and all the verses to each hymn during every service. It was through the hymns that I began to learn about the character of the Lord. I had a very good Sunday School teacher who challenged us about the importance of God's Word in our lives. I was an avid reader and my pastor had a good library of Christian novels. I read all they had and learned a lot from the books that were for younger readers like the Danny Orlis series. One book had a big impact on my life, but the funny thing was I lost interest in that book and did not finish it. The thing that impressed me in the story was that the main character was told she should read the Bible and start with the book of John. I hadn't realized we were to read the Bible on our own so I started reading the book of John. That is when my relationship with the Lord really took off. I loved the Bible and would read on and on into the night. My pastor's son was my age and we had known each other since kindergarten. We became good friends and he explained so much about the Lord and the Bible that I did not know. The Lord really used that special friendship in my life to help me grow as a believer.

Something else the Lord really used in my life was a program that my church joined every year with Bible Memory Association. It was a 12-week program where we would memorize one lesson of Bible verses a week and then quote it to a "hearer" in the church each Sunday. We chose our rewards from a catalog, which had Bibles, study helps, books and Bible games. Since I was in high school I had to memorize 14 verses a week. The curriculum started with preschoolers and went up to adults. It was a great program! I am so glad I was encouraged to memorize the Scripture at that time in my life.

A turning point in my life came as a result of a phone conversation with my pastor's son. I had been reading the book of Revelations and I asked him,

> "Why does it say that '*God will wipe all the tears from our eyes.*' We will be in Heaven where everything is great - why will people be crying?"

> He paused and then said, "*It is because they have lived their lives for themselves and not for the Lord.*"

It was like a sword pierced my heart! I realized that I had not done anything for the Lord and was living for myself. That summer before I entered 9th grade, I gave my life over to the Lord and never looked back.

Needless to say, my family was not all that excited about me becoming a "religious fanatic". I had no encouragement from them to follow the Lord and at times, they opposed my faith and me.

All through 11th grade I was praying the Lord would show me what to do with my life. I was just a farm girl with no great talents to give Him. I never considered anything else but some full-time ministry, but I had no clue what it would be.

The summer after 11th grade I was talking to my girlfriend's mother on the phone and she told me that their youth group was going to Canada to visit a family from their church that was going through missionary training with New Tribes Mission. Her youth group was going to visit the missionary family and attend the missionary conference there. She encouraged me to go with them. The funny thing is my mom would not allow me to go on a outing with my youth group which was not that far away, but she allowed me go to Canada with my girlfriend's youth group.

I had never met a missionary before and knew absolutely nothing about missions. The songs and the messages I heard really pierced my heart! I found out about the huge need for missionaries, how Christians are commanded in God's Word to spread the Gospel and that God uses the weak and foolish things of the world. As a result of going to that missionary conference (we were only there for two days), I believed the Lord wanted me to be a missionary. The Lord used people and circumstances to clearly guide me to start training with New Tribes Mission. My parents were not happy at all about my decision and told me they would not support my decision. The Lord gave me a good paying job at the post office right across from the New Tribes Bible School. I was able to earn enough to pay my three semesters of Bible School.

It was during my second semester that a shy boy from Lancaster County started Bible School. Galen and I were just friends and when I finished Bible school I went to the next phase of the training which is now called Mission Institute. I went to the one in Canada - the place where I was challenged to be a missionary. When it was time for Galen to move into the second phase of training, he requested to go to the school in Florida. He was sent to - guess where - Canada! It was during my two years of training in Canada that Galen and I fell in love and were married.

We entered the last phase of training after only being married a few months. This phase was in Missouri and for us only lasted one semester. This was language school where we learned all the sounds your mouth can make and how to write down a language just by the sounds you hear, how to go about learning a language and culture, literacy and some medical classes. After a year of partnership building, we left for the Philippines with our 7-month-old daughter, Maria. Shane was born during our first term as missionaries on the field and Chris was born during our second term on the field.

When we went to the Philippines our idea of missionary life was that we would live in a remote tribal village, learn the language and serve the Lord there for 20 plus years and see a strong church established. Our goal was to work ourselves out of a job. Well, for the Martin family it really didn't work out that way.

During our first term on the field, we moved into a very remote village that had no roads to get there. We went in and out using the small missionary airplane that serviced the missionaries on the island of Luzon. Our grass airstrip was about 2 miles from the village and you had to climb up to the top of a ridge to get to it. The way we handle Bible study is we teach chronologically through the Bible. When Galen was finishing up teaching Genesis a tribal war started over the ownership of land. We had to flee because it was way too dangerous to stay in the village. We had been on the field 4 years and even though we would have liked to have a five-year term, we decided this would be a good time to give things time to resolve themselves. Little did we know that the conflict would last for many years and many people would be killed.

When we returned to start our second term on the field it was obvious we could not return to working with the Isnag people. There was a couple working in a tribe with a language that was very close that wanted partners. So we joined them and started learning the language there, which was really just a different dialect of the language we already knew. We knew our time in this village would be short - maybe two years. It was a very "hot" area with communist guerillas coming through all the time. After being with this couple for three months in the tribe they decided they would rather serve the Lord in Manila so they left and we were on our own again.

For Galen and I, those two years in that village were the most difficult we ever had. The pressure of being in the middle of a war zone and the apathy of the believers that Galen tried to minister to made it very discouraging. Then on June 1, 1987, a huge group of guerillas filled the village. We had radio contact that day and using a code we were taught, we communicated with our support center that the guerillas were in the village and had made contact with us. We had no idea that <u>we</u> were the purpose of their visit. To make a long story short, they held Galen at gunpoint under our house while they ransacked our home. The first thing they took was our short wave radio, which cut off any contact we had with the outside world. I was up in the house with our three children and watched them go through everything. When they finally left I was almost in tears, but Galen - can you believe this - came up all smiles because he was able to negotiate with the guerillas to give us back our box of slides that we kept in an old army ammo box!

We did not sleep that night and some of the believers sneaked over to talk to us. The guerillas told us to leave and actually, I was really glad to do just that! It was decided that we would leave over land the next morning. We still had our motorcycle.

I would like to add here that the Lord did something very special for me to prepare me for what we were going through. The 1980's were very difficult years in the Philippines. A lot of our missionaries were in very difficult situations and some had to leave their tribes for a period of time. One family who worked on another island had - just the year before - the same thing happen to them. The guerillas ransacked their house and told them to leave. Our mission has an annual missionary conference every year where all the missionaries get together for a time of teaching and fellowship. It is like a family reunion as some of us who work on other islands only get to see each other once a year. While we were at our guesthouse in Manila at conference time, I happened to visit with the lady who had their home ransacked by the guerillas. She told me the whole story of what happened to them and how they felt going through that experience. The Lord used that time with her to prepare my heart for what we were going to experience months after my visit with her. By the way, they were able to return to their village and continue to serve the Lord there.

The next morning the support center called us for a weather check as we were to have a flight that day but we never came by. They had *no* idea what had happened to us.

Just at daybreak, I left the village with Maria and our neighbor came with me and strapped my baby Chris on his back. We walked about an hour before Galen came with the motorcycle and 3-year-old Shane. The first part of the trip out was too rough for Galen to have anyone on the bike so that is why we hiked. For the next four hours the five of us rode the cycle a little and walked when the trail was too washed out. When we reached a town the kids and I road a jeepney, which is a type of public transportation, and Galen went ahead on the cycle. Once we got to a bigger town Galen phoned our Manila office and told them in code what happened.

As a family, we lived at the support center for two months trying to decide what to do. The Lord led us to relocate at the provincial capital of the province we had been living in. The tribal people would come out to us and we would minister to them as we could. During that time I became very ill. It was like I had malaria all the time. We decided to go home to the United States and try to get me some help. We took a two-year medical furlough. The doctors could not find anything wrong with me even though I was so ill. I know now that it was fibromyalgia but it would be over 10 years before I would find that out.

During our extended furlough, Galen got training in electronics and we spent the last seven months of our home assignment in Arizona where he was able to get more training on avionics. We returned to the field for our third term and lived at the center that was our support center when we were in the tribe. Galen fixed radios and worked on the airplane radio and anything to do with it. Our kids went to the mission school, which was on the compound and loved it there. There was a dorm full of kids and lots of neighbors. The center was a fantastic place for kids. Those were good years even though they had their own challenges too.

At the end of our four-year term Galen and another missionary hiked into the first village we had worked in during the 1980's. They came back with the wonderful news that the tribal land war was over and it was safe for us to return to that area. We went on furlough with the mindset of preparing to return to the tribe again after being gone from that village for 13 years. We never were able to present the Gospel there and always wanted to return.

The Lord provided a new radioman to take Galen's place. In January of 1997, another missionary came to help Galen remove 30-foot trees that had grown on our airstrip since we had left. After months of hard work, the airstrip was finished and we returned to the village of Maragat and started our work again with the Isnage people.

Skipping ahead to 2003, Galen and I were out of the tribe for our annual missionary conference in March. Galen had been coughing for months in the tribe and was actually not as energetic as he normally was. To make a long story short, we had him checked out in Manila and they found cancer cells from the fluid they drew from his lung and a scan showed a mass in his left lung.

It was unthinkable that this would happen to Galen. He was always so healthy and strong. We went home shortly after we found out and the Lord gave us a year with Galen. The Lord was so good to give our family time to regroup. Maria was with the Peace Corps in Africa and Shane was in Bible school in Wisconsin. Chris finished out his school year in the Philippines and joined us a few months later.

Galen responded well to the chemotherapy. We needed a home and decided to trust the Lord to build a home - our first in the United States. Our home was a huge blessing as it gave our family a wonderful place to spend Galen's remaining time together.

I will never forget when our doctor had to tell us that the cancer had gone to his brain and there was a lot of it. I saw his scans and they were full of white patches where the cancer was growing. It was then that I had to face the fact that I was going to be a widow. What a terrible night that was for me as I stayed with Galen in the hospital. He was released in a few days and received radiation treatment as an outpatient for a few weeks. It wasn't long after that the Galen I knew for 25 years was no more. The Lord gave me the grace to accept this new Galen and to take care of him. In Proverbs it says, "*Even in death, the righteous have a refuge.*" We were Galen's refuge as we took care of him. He became more weak and confused. We were so thankful for Hospice and all the wonderful support they gave us in taking care of Galen at home. On May 27, 2004, Galen went Home to be with the Lord. We were all with him in our home as he took his last breath. He had been so sick, I was wanting him to go and be with the Lord.

The Lord had been showing me all along that I could trust Him and that He would give me wisdom and would lead me. He is such a good teacher! I must admit that my first year without Galen was very hard. I cried a lot as things seemed so overwhelming at times. All I can say is the Lord got me through it and He used His Word and many dear believers to come alongside and help me out

I would like to add this little story to show you how good the Lord was to me. When Galen was in the hospital in Baltimore, some friends brought me home so I could shower, rest and change my clothes. After they left me at my house I was throwing away the trash in the garage when I realized I was locked out of the house. The door going to the garage would open from the inside so you would not realize that it was locked until you shut it and you were locked out. We had just moved into our house about a month before and I didn't really know my neighbors yet. It was February, nighttime and I was barefoot. I just sat down on the steps and cried out to the Lord. *What do I do now?* We were going to make the area over our garage into an apartment and it had steps leading down to the garage and had a door in it that went into the upstairs hall. I felt the Lord wanted me to go up to that area which had lots of things including tools in it. I went up and it seemed the Lord told me to take the hinges from the door so I could get back inside the house. Well, I did that and was able to get back in the house. The Lord showed me that night that He would never leave me or forsake me and I could always trust in Him.

My goal was to return to work in the tribe. Without Galen I was not sure if I had value by myself as a missionary. The Lord was very gracious to me each step of the way. My partners were very supportive of me rejoining them in the village. When I did finally return to the tribe in October of 2005, I still was not sure if I would fit in by myself. It did not take long for me to see that yes, the Lord could still use me as I was -even without Galen. It was not easy, but I found the Lord constantly going before me and preparing the way. He helped me remember important things when I needed that information. He guided me and basically "looked out" for me in big and small details.

This year marks my fourth year in the tribe and I am so amazed how God has used me. I had been praying for years that I would be able to teach health classes to the women. In October of 2005 I was working in the clinic one day and after spending some time one-on-one with one of the women teaching her things she needed to know, I turned to my helper who is also is a tribal lady and said, "We need a mothers' class!" She agreed so we sat down and planned what we wanted to teach. The mothers' class was a great success! Now I do not teach it anymore. I have four tribal ladies I meet with once a week and go over the lesson and they are teaching it.

Vicky holding the newborn of another Isnag mother last year

At the same time one of the believers asked me if I would teach a women's Bible study when rice harvest is over. We started meeting in one of the tribal homes once a week and started in Genesis. I taught chronologically through the Bible and we just finished the life of Christ in March of this year. Now I have seven women I meet with on Monday night to go over the lesson that is taught on Thursday night, to pray together and study the Bible. It has been such a joy to see these ladies grow in their understanding of God's Word and in their walk with the Lord. It is like icing on the cake to me to spend time with them in God's Word.

Last year, the family that was working here in the tribe moved to Manila so their kids could go to middle school and high school at Faith Academy. That left just Robbie, a nurse who runs the clinic and myself in the tribe. In November of last year the Lord worked in the lives of 7 men who wanted to be taught the Bible so they could teach it on Sunday afternoon here in the village. We had prayed for years for some men to step up to the plate. In this culture, the men tend to sit back and let the women do everything. So I find myself discipling a group of men and teaching them to be teachers. It is exciting to see their desire to be taught and to teach. They also are going to a village an hour hike downstream to teach the Bible. This has been a real encouragement to their faith to do this.

I am so humbled that He would use me, even as a widow, to serve Him in this little isolated village in Northern Luzon. To God be all the Glory!

Chapter Thirteen:
God Is Faithful and Trustworthy
By Deane C. Bell

"Trust in the Lord with all your heart,
And lean not on your own understanding;
In all your ways acknowledge Him,
And He shall direct your paths."
Proverbs 3:5-6

I was born April 3, 1932, in Lansing, Michigan. I graduated from Eastern High School and Lansing Business University. I was also in the Naval Reserves for 8 years. My parents were good to me and my younger brother, Jim, who now lives in Florida. At age 7, my mother became ill with a crippling disease. This created quite a burden on our family. We had to dress her, do dishes, and do the housework. My mother died at the age of 53 after being ill for 20 years. My father's dedication to her was admirable. Her illness taught me many lessons, which help me today to empathize with people less fortunate than I. We had a good secular home, but it was void of any prayer or spiritual life. However, our parents truly loved us and taught us good values. I will always be thankful to the Lord for them.

Due to my mother's condition, I spent summers in northern Michigan on my grandparents' farm. Those were enjoyable times. I probably developed my belief in God there – primarily in the open fields as I gazed at the beautiful sky. In my teens, mutual friends attended the Methodist Church and I had the desire to play on their basketball team. I attended the Methodist Church, but the Word (the Bible) did not penetrate. At least I was exposed to some Christian truths. Sports were of great interest to me as a young teenager, especially baseball, although I did enjoy both basketball and football too. Golf came later.

In 1953, I was married, and in 1954 I converted to Roman Catholicism. In one year, I learned more about religion than I had in the first 21 years of my life. During this time we had two sons and three daughters. I became very active in the Catholic Church and in its defense. My 5 children were brought up in Catholic school and I was happy. I felt at peace with God. I sensed my family was in the only true church going in the direction that God desired. My work as an accountant at Farm Bureau Insurance Company was enjoyable and challenging.

In the summer of 1969 – POW! There was trouble developing and my marriage was disintegrating. I felt as if my little world was crumbling. I sought council and I searched my soul. This was a very traumatic period in my life. An approximate 5-month separation took place and a try at reconciliation for 6 months after that.

Many times I cried to God. I began to question my faith and for the first time, I commenced questioning my Catholic belief. I determined that never again would I allow any one or any church to dictate my conscience. Eventually, I left the Catholic Church even though my thoughts concerning it were mixed.

Although I didn't know it, God was leading me through this stressful period. My marriage eventually ended in divorce. I am still a firm believer that God intended marriage to be a lifetime commitment. Perhaps God hates and warns against divorce because of the pain it causes and the moral breakdown it brings to His world.

Life continued and God is good. I was determined to go forward hoping that God would give me direction. In the fall of 1970, my future wife, Betty came to Michigan with her parents and grandmother. My ex-mother-in-law invited me to dinner because they were at her home. This was a unique situation which I will not go into detail at this time. My first impression when I saw Betty was – WOW! We packed in three full days of seeing each other, and I was walking on air. We had conversations covering many areas including spiritual commitments. I made many trips to PA before we were married June 19, 1971 at a Baptist Church in New Britain, Pennsylvania.

After we married we moved to St Johns, Michigan. We were nearly broke, but we loved each other and I had my job. What more did we need? Betty and I had many spiritual discussions, but where we would attend church was the big question. Betty was saved in a Baptist Church and I was Roman Catholic. The Methodist Church was our compromise choice. We did have ministers from various churches come and visit us. I must admit that only the Baptist minister impressed me, but I had some hang-ups with Baptists.

Around this time, I was reading the book by Hal Lindsey, "*The Late Great Planet Earth*". Betty and I also went to a Leighton Ford (Billy Graham's associate) Reach-out in Lansing. I went forward, but I wasn't saved at this time. I was only in a transition period. They gave me a correspondence course in the book of John, which I completed. Meanwhile, Betty and others were praying for me.

One Sunday, Betty was sick and I went to church alone, but instead of going to the Methodist Church, I went to the Baptist Church and we continued to pursue that direction. Since leaving the Catholic Church, I refuse to play the denominational game, although I do have leanings toward certain denominations. I usually tell people that I'm a Christian who attends a fundamental Bible-believing church.

I was saved in May 1973, and baptized in October 1973. The Holy Spirit used the Word of God and people praying behind the scenes to bring about these events in my life. By God's grace, I made the greatest decision I have ever made in my life. It says in Romans 10:17 "*So then faith cometh by hearing, and hearing by the word of God*". When the Word gets in you, it makes a difference. As a former Catholic, the verses that had the most impact on me were Ephesians 2:8-9 "*For by grace are ye saved through faith; and that not of ourselves, it is the gift of God—not of works, lest any man should boast*". There were many other verses that the Holy Spirit used to convict me such as Titus 3:5 and Acts 4:12. The Word of God broke down many prior barriers that I had by being Catholic. I realized that I am redeemed only by the blood of Jesus and not by any effort on my part. His outpouring of love to me is beyond my understanding, but this great gift I have accepted with all my heart and with thanksgiving. I have appreciated the various ministers of the Gospel that I have sat under and the teachings of the scholars whose writings I have read. The Holy Spirit has convicted me concerning the truth of God's Word.

We became members of the First Baptist Church in St Johns, Michigan and served there for 26 years. I served as assistant treasurer, building treasurer, usher, missionary committee, assisting with teaching college and career classes. I was one of four people who wrote the missionary policy at our church. Betty and I have had the privilege of having visiting pastors and missionaries in our home many times. We also had counsel with some people in our home. On two separate occasions we had teen-aged girls stay in our home for months.

In 1995, I retired from Farm Bureau Insurance as tax manager after 40 years of service. I was glad to get out of the fast lane. In those many years, I worked with many outstanding people. Just a few months before I retired, I had my first heart attack. I recovered well—at least for about 4 years.

One of our former pastors, Tom Dolph and his wife Jean, invited us to Maranatha Village in December 1996. This is a Christian Village in Sebring, FL. January through March 1998, we rented a mobile home. We fell in love with the people in Maranatha Village. The week of March 1998, we purchased a doublewide home. We made many friends and thought this would be our home for years to come. However, in July 2006, Betty and I left Maranatha Village to be caregivers to Betty's mother in New Holland, PA, after she gave us an S.O.S call for help. As of this writing, her mother is 89, a diabetic with congestive heart failure. It wasn't easy leaving our many friends in Maranatha after living there 7 years. I served as an usher, moderator at morning devotions, auditor of the church finances and auditor at The Manor, an assisted living home facility. I assisted others in visiting people in nursing homes and hospitals on various occasions. I was also involved in Village night security, treasurer of the golf league, and helped with maintaining the on-sight unique golf course.

My spiritual life grew at Maranatha. I had two major heart attacks, in 1999 and 2004, and in 2004 I experienced cardiac arrest. The years 2004 and 2005 were tough physical years as after my heart attack, I had a pace maker and defibrillator installed. I suffered with double pneumonia, experienced an upper GI endoscopy, colonoscopy, polymyalgia rheumatica, shingles, and had cataract surgery. Needless to say, I had quite a few serious conversations with the Lord during that time. God was always faithful and patient with me. In our Village, I had three close mentors – two former pastors, and an inspiring spiritual leader. These godly men were either in their late 80's or early 90's and were excellent sources of wisdom to me. There were many golfing buddies I played with and got close to. This Christian Village was very special to me. It was difficult leaving, but life is full of adjustments and it is best to be content when the Lord is directing your path.

Betty and I have had many blessings in our marriage for nearly 38 years. She is not only my wife, sweetheart, and friend, but also my confidant. Without Betty's help and encouragement, I would have never made it through my health difficulties. To me, she is a portrait of the virtuous woman of Proverbs 31. We have a commitment to one another and to our Lord. God is amazing, always good and always right. He is behind the scenes controlling the scenes that He is behind.

Since our arrival to Pennsylvania in July of 2006, we have attended Christian Fellowship Church. We think highly of the people here and recognize that God's Word is being preached. It is our prayer that God will continue to bless this church body abundantly.

Chapter Fourteen:
Pursued by God
By Heather Sherman

*"For I am confident of this very thing,
that He who began a good work in you will perfect it
until the day of Christ Jesus."*
Philippians 1:6

Growing up, I was one of "those" kids: raised in a Christian home, involved in church, sent to Christian school; you know the type. I knew how to play the part so well. I knew all of the Bible stories and had the answers to all of the questions. But, I lacked a true relationship with God, and I lacked confidence in my faith. I was-- and still am-- a people pleaser. Along the way, that attribute has caused much heartache for me and has led me away from God at several points in my life.

As I grew more independent in high school, I realized I didn't really know who I was or where I was going. I wasn't secure in myself and I certainly wasn't secure in my relationship with God. In tenth grade, during a Spiritual Life Conference led by Keith Walker, I re-dedicated my life for the umpteenth time. During that conference, Keith focused on I Timothy 1:7 which says, "*For God did not give us a spirit of timidity [fear], but a spirit of power, of love and of self-discipline.*" I have come back to that verse many times wondering why it never took hold. It did take hold, in some small way, because I look back and realize that was the first time I actually felt and recognized the Holy Spirit. Unfortunately, the emotional high of that conference didn't last long and I eventually closed my ears to anything the Holy Spirit had to say. It would be ten years before I opened my ears and heart to the Spirit again.

A year out of high school, I hadn't committed to going to college. I was working the bare minimum, and I was acting irresponsibly. After a tumultuous year with some broken hearts and wounds that I would carry well into my future, I was introduced to an incredible guy who was in a band with a friend I'd known in high school. He was sweet and funny and was at a similar place in life. We were both superficial Christians, unsteady in our spirituality, and our existence. I had not dated at all in high school, and at 19, Jason was my first boyfriend. There were certain things I thought I believed and knew about dating. But I was naive. Jason & I talked about marriage soon after we started dating, but were only half-serious about it. We fooled around in the way we were both taught not to, but because of our lack of relationship with God; we were not convicted to follow His plan for us. We'd go too far; one of us would feel guilty; we'd back off. It was a vicious cycle. In October, five months after we'd started dating, I took a pregnancy test and found out I was going to have a baby. At that time, I honestly couldn't have predicted children anywhere in my future -- especially not at 19!

Over the next few weeks, we decided to plan a wedding for February. We'd have about 5 months together as husband and wife before the baby was born. I've heard people say that the first year of marriage is the most difficult. Strangely enough, in spite of the circumstances under which we entered into marriage, our first year was, in some ways, easier than the ones that would follow.

Jason & Heather

Our son was about a year old when Jason decided to start a band with his brother. Little did we know what that band would lead to. At first, they just played a few shows here and there. Gradually, they increased their fan base and played shows at the Chameleon (a club) semi-frequently. For a while, we were able to maintain both a somewhat normal life and a party life. We always found a sitter for our son, Ben, so we could both go to shows. At this point, we were both 21, so we could drink, and more often than not, we opted to both drink instead of having a designated driver. The more Jason's band played the club, the more people in the "scene" we surrounded ourselves with. We were so far from God, and yet His protection was on us every time we went to a show, every time we drank and then chose to drive home, every time we put ourselves in a situation we knew we shouldn't be in. After several years of our drinking, partying and, most unfortunately, cheating on each other more than once, the drummer in Jason's band announced that he was done with the band. Rather than searching for another drummer, which was normally how Jason handled that sort of thing, he chose to dissolve the band. Even in the drummer's decision to quit, God's hand was at work; it was one of the best decisions God made for us.

About a month after the last show, we were hit with a huge attack on our marriage when the secrets we had been hiding from each other were revealed. We admitted our sins to each other and then we begged each other for forgiveness. Then, we turned to God confessing our sins to Him and begging His forgiveness. We both quickly realized how far we were from God, but He drew us to Him instantly. Once we confessed our sins, we committed ourselves, our marriage, and our family to God. We gave them all to Him knowing that He was the only one who could heal our wounds.

Another month after that, one of our close friends was in an accident that was a result of drunk driving. The tragedy of that accident, the terribleness of what happened to her, opened our eyes even more to the path we'd been on, the path from which God had protected us and then removed us. He changed the course of our lives even in the midst of our ignorance, and He waited patiently for us to realize that He was at work in us from the start.

More than anything I've realized that God had been protecting us all along, long before we chose to acknowledge Him as Savior. He protected our son by giving us loving families who took care of him while we were being irresponsible. He maintained the bond of our marriage when one or both of us desecrated it and tried to walk away. We both still have wounds caused by that lifestyle, and there are things I can't ever forgive myself for, but everyday I thank God for pursuing me in endless ways and for protecting my marriage and my family in spite of my constant disregard for His love and His plan for my life. He provided outlets for me and ways for me to escape the life I was leading, but I continually ignored His attempts to save me from the world.

I look back now knowing that I've made some horrible choices in my life. I also know that God pursued me in spite of my choices; He used those choices for the greater good in my life. He used those choices to bring me to His throne where I could collapse in despair and fatigue and fear, and then, He took my burdens from me and said *"Child, you are forgiven."* The pursuit was the hardest part, and now I am finally living in God's glory.

I know that this is only the beginning of my journey, and that I have much to learn about truly being a daughter of God and allowing Him to write my story - to complete it in His time. As I grow in His love and in His grace, I find myself drawn to the Psalms for comfort, such as Psalm 13:5&6 *"But I trust in Your unfailing love; my heart rejoices in Your salvation. I will sing to the Lord for he has been good to me."* There was no reason for God to spare my life or family and yet, I am here today, able to share with others what He has done for me. My spirit also finds respite in Galatians 2:20 (NIV), *"I have been crucified with Christ, and I no longer live, but Christ lives in me. The life I live in the body I live by faith in the son of God who loved me and gave Himself for me."* I am grateful for the transformation that took place in my life, and I am confident that the God who started this great work in me will be faithful to complete it.

Jason, Ben & Heather

Chapter Fifteen:

Memories that Last a Lifetime

By Mary Lou Good

"My brethren, count it all joy when ye fall into various trials, knowing that the testing of your faith produces endurance."
James 1:2-3

I am writing this in honor of our Lord Jesus Christ and to pay tribute of how He saved a sinner such as I, Mary Lou (Jenkins) Good.

The Bible says in John 3:16 *"For God so loved the world that He gave His only begotten Son, that whosoever believeth in him should not perish, but have everlasting life."*

I was born August 5, 1944, to Everett Gibson Jenkins and Rebecca Mae Jenkins. I was raised in Lancaster, Pennsylvania. I have a twin sister, Donna Lee, and I have two older brothers: Bob, 8 years older and Dave, 3 years older. We were very poor, at least we thought we were. However, we always had clean clothing, food on the table - not always meat and potatoes - but my mother could make the best corn-fritters.

We owned our own home in Lancaster and that was bought on a handshake, that my daddy would pay every month, which he did. He borrowed the money from Ben Weaver, his boss at Shirk's Motor Express. There was always foul language spoken, smoking, and drinking in our family, but that was the norm for us. Growing up, I was so embarrassed with all this and as a teenager, I vowed I would never marry a man that did those kinds of things.

My mother sent me to work at the age of ten cleaning the neighbors' homes. One neighbor made me a skirt out of a feedbag, and I thought it was so neat. I gave all the money I earned, which wasn't much, to my mother. I attended Edward Hand Junior High School and was chosen to sing in the choir. One year I had a special part in a choir event. I wanted a new dress for that event, but we were so poor that I didn't think I could get it. Mother found a way to buy a pretty dress, but no shoes to go with it. So the neighbor lent me a pair of shoes. They were a half a size too small, but I made them do. My mother took in 13 washing (laundry) jobs for people and my daddy worked 2 jobs to keep our family going.

My childhood may have been poor materially speaking, but it was rich with friends and family. Our father would always take us away on the weekends, after he was finished working. My parents were very good parents, playing ball at the park (Long's Park) ice skating, sledding, picnicking, going to the bay (Crystal Beach Manor in Maryland) swimming, having people over, or just visiting people. I was amazed at all the energy my daddy had.

We had an elderly neighbor lady, Mom-Mom Witmer, who was a big influence in my life. She invited Donna Lee and me over to her home many times and we learned to sing old hymns together as she would play the piano. Our family was not a church-going family. If it wouldn't have been for Mom-Mom, Donna Lee and I wouldn't have gone to church at all. But Mom-Mom got the minister, Mr. Sam Sheaffer, to pick us up in his car and together they'd take us to Sunday School at East End Chapel Church every Sunday. While there, we learned about Jesus and sang together with Mom-Mom at the piano. After Sunday School, Mr. Sheaffer gave us a candy bar just for coming. (That was a real treat for us because Mother would only give us a penny to buy a piece of candy!) We learned to love this old gentleman, Mr. Sheaffer. He taught us verses to memorize every Sunday. We started going to church with him when we were about 5 years old and went there until we were teenagers. My father never came with us to church, but Mother would come sometimes. I accepted Jesus Christ into my heart on November 29, 1953.

When I was 12, I asked Mr. Sheaffer if there was somebody - a guy - out there just for me and he said, "*Yes. Someone very special.*" That's when I started going to dances at school, fire halls and even some churches. My mother and daddy were always dancing to Lawrence Welk while watching him on television on Saturday nights. Then daddy would ask Donna and me to dance with him. We would have wonderful times doing that. Donna and I learned to jitterbug really well. We had this down to a routine.

During my teenage years, I walked away from church, but I always knew what I wanted in my life. It was a good life, but something was missing. I was sliding back into my old ways since there was little guidance for church. I started dating at the age of 15. I had a goal of only dating Christian guys who didn't smoke, drink or use foul language. This was something my father told me, even though he would not go to church with us. He was strict about the fellows we dated. Since Donna and I were twins, we sounded a lot alike on the phone, so when the guys would call us, we would pretend we were the other and get a laugh out of that! I dated a lot of nice guys and went to dances, but I knew I was missing one thing: a relationship with our Lord Jesus Christ. If you are born into a Christian home with a good foundation, you can be very thankful. But if you are not, life is a struggle.

It was challenging growing up in the city where all kinds of crime surrounded us. Fighting was one of the biggest things I feared. Edward Hand was one of the roughest schools that I went to; I was afraid all the time. The girls instigated fights to see how well I could fight back. I am not proud of what I did, especially when forced to beat up another girl. I was frightened, but my friends looked out for me at school. In spite of the fighting, I was a good student and got on the honor roll. I even ran around with a nice crowd of friends. But there were always trials to face. I was so glad to get out of that school and move on. I graduated from J.P. McCaskey High School in 1963.

During my high school years, I dated Raymond (my future husband) - a student from Pequea Valley High School. He had a true testimony of the kind of man that I wanted to marry. He was gentle and kind. Often, we would talk about the Lord. When dating

Raymond & Mary Lou dating in 1962

Raymond, I had to go to church with him every Sunday. I got tired of this and went back to dating other nice guys. I loved to dance, but Raymond didn't. I knew that all of the other guys didn't have the love in their heart for the Lord like Raymond did, so 3 months after breaking it off with Raymond, we got back together. Raymond called me on December 27, 1961, and said that he thought we should get back together and I said, "*Okay!*" We started dating again, and I found myself willing to go to church with him. We joined Neffsville Mennonite Church, but my parents wouldn't come to see us taken into membership. Raymond's parents, Harvey and Katie Good, came and that meant a lot to me. After dating 2½ years, we were married at Neffsville Mennonite and had our wedding reception at Plain and Fancy Restaurant.

About 2 years later we had our daughter, Dawn Renee Good. We lived in Intercourse, Pennsylvania. I can't say that those years were easy; I was caught between my family and Raymond's family. Even though Raymond was an only child, we were constantly visited by his parents and told what to do and what to buy. Every holiday was spent with his family. Every Friday night we would have a nice time visiting my family. We certainly didn't see eye-to-eye on things - they drank, smoked and used foul language. We never drank with them because they knew where we stood on that issue. There were times we were made fun of and told to leave. But whenever one of my family members had a problem, they always called us to see what they should do. Through all of this, I loved my mother and father. My father even signed the papers so we could buy our first home in Intercourse, Pennsylvania, in 1968.

In April 1971, we started attending Christian Fellowship Church (CFC), which met at Millstream Motor Lodge in Smoketown, Pennsylvania. Pastor Irvin Martin and his loving wife, Irene, helped us make the change from Neffsville Mennonite Church to CFC. The Martins were wonderful mentors to us - 2 young people and their daughter. We would have great talks with them and there was a bond of friendship that grew out of Christian love for each other. Pastor Irvin Martin asked Jean Martin, Mabel Weaver, and me to sing at our first Easter at CFC. It was a wonderful fellowship we had with one another - we were a church family.

Eight years after Dawn was born we had our son, Curtis Lamar Good. Lamar is Raymond's middle name. We were so pleased that we finally had a son to carry on our Good name, and Dawn was so proud of her little brother. Everyone at church was happy for us. We had so many fun times with our church family, it was small then and we all knew and visited each other. I finally had examples of Christian people. I loved our church family and grew in the Word of our Lord Jesus Christ. You could see the changes in my life and my love for our Savior.

In the early years of CFC, I taught Sunday School, Vacation Bible School, was in the choir, and was the church decorator for about 25 years. A few years ago, I asked Grace Martin and Charlene Shreiner to help me with the decorating. Raymond and I have really enjoyed serving the Lord in so many ways.

Our children were growing up, so I started working at Erb's Market in New Holland. I worked in the office during the evening. A lot of young kids worked there. I know now why the Lord put me there. The kids and I became very close and we would talk about the Lord. They were having rough times and they knew that I would be there for them. I could share so many stories with you, but this one gal there was being pulled between the Lord and Satan. She was in school and trying so hard to find her way. So I shared about what the Lord had done in my life and how He could work in hers. She had about the same background that I did. She needed someone to talk to and as I look back today, I can see how the Lord played a big part in my life all the time.

This is one of my favorite songs and this passage is so deeply loved, and is known by all.

"The Lord is my shepherd" and "I am His sheep."
The Twenty-third Psalm
The Lord is my shepherd;
I shall not want.
He makes me to lie down in green pastures;
He leads me beside the still waters.
He restores my soul;
He leads me in the path of righteousness

For His name's sake.
Yea, though I walk through the valley of the
Shadow of death, I will fear no evil;
Your rod and Your staff, they comfort me.
You prepare a table before me in the presence of my enemies;
You anoint my head with oil;
My cup runs over.
Surely goodness and mercy shall follow me
All the days of my life;
And I will dwell in the house of the LORD FOREVER.

In Romans 3:23 it says, "*For all have sinned and fall short of the glory of God.*" In Romans 6:23 it says, "*For the wages of sin is death, but the gift of God is eternal life in Christ Jesus our Lord.*" In John 3:3 Jesus said, "*Truly, truly, I say to you, unless one is born again, he can not see the kingdom of God.*" John 14:6 "*I am the way and the truth, and the life; no one comes to the Father, but through Me.*"

I learned all of these verses when I was a child. As I shared the plan of salvation with this young gal at work, she had questions. If I didn't know the answers, I always took the time and found them, and we would talk again. I had to quit that job because of back surgery. I saw that gal many years later at Green Dragon Farmers Market in Ephrata, Pennsylvania, and she came running up to me, asking if I remembered her. When I called her by name – Fran - we hugged. She told me that if it wouldn't have been for me taking time with her, that she didn't know where she would be. She is married to a young man in ministry and has accepted the Lord Jesus Christ as her Savior. She is very passionate about her relationship with the Lord. I told Fran I was so proud of her - how she has turned her life around - and I told her that I loved her in the Lord. You never know who is watching or listening to you, but that was the Lord working in me.

It was around this time that my father became ill with a stroke and was admitted into the Lancaster General Hospital. Raymond and I had been praying for him for over 20 years. Ten days before he died he accepted the Lord Jesus Christ into his heart. Our Lord was faithful to the end. My father was praising the Lord right up until he died. *Oh, how I wished I had that as a child.* Ten years later my mother went home to be with the Lord. Before she died she asked me to let her go. She said she was praying all day and made everything right with the Lord and wanted me to give her the "okay" to pass onto her heavenly Home. I hugged her and we cried together. I told her when Christ is ready He will come and take her Home. The very next morning at 5:30, she passed into eternity. The Lord heard our prayers and was faithful. Those final days I spent with my parents were very precious to me. My parents knew Raymond and I were always there for them no matter what and that we loved them.

On April 1, 2008, I had bilateral knee surgery. The Lord was right there the whole time - *He will never leave you or forsake you.* It was major surgery and I could feel His presence and know that all of our friends were praying for me. All the Bible verses I learned as a child kept flowing back to me. My surgeon, Dr. Thomas Westphal, said I was amazing. I told him it wasn't me but the faith that I have in the Lord Jesus Christ that has carried me through. It was also the prayers of our friends.

Dawn, Lynn, Isaac, Liz & Noah Shertzer

Our children are grown now, Dawn is married to Pastor Lynn Shertzer, a Mennonite minister at Slate Hill Mennonite Church in Camp Hill, Pennsylvania. They have blessed us with 3 grandchildren, Isaac (16), Liz (15) and Noah (12). They live in Mechanicsburg, Pennsylvania. Our son, Curtis, is married to Andrea (Blank) Good and they have blessed us with 2 more grandsons, Tristan (11) and Quillan (8). They own a farm in Quarryville, Pennsylvania, and are members of Strasburg Mennonite Church in Strasburg, Pennsylvania. We are so thankful for our dear little family and what they have accomplished over the years. We have raised them in a "Good" Christian home and can see the fruits of His teaching. They are a blessing to us.

Curtis, Andrea, Tristan & Quillan Good

February 15, 2009, marked 45 years that Raymond and I were married. I love him as much today as I did when we were married. We are still sweethearts.

The Lord has done marvelous things for me and He can do that for you, too. Invite Jesus Christ into your heart, ask Him for forgiveness of your sins and become a child of His. It is a free gift. Don't let this day go by without knowing the Lord Jesus Christ as your Savior. Faithfulness is rewarded: "Your Will, Not Mine." Always remember Christians aren't perfect, just forgiven.

Chapter Sixteen:

God Healed My Broken Heart

By Eve Woodward*

"The grass is always greener over the septic tank!"
-Erma Bombeck

*Fictional name is used to protect author's identity

I have been attending Christian Fellowship Church (CFC) for nearly six years. Many folks at church do not know my past and I rarely talk about it. I was asked to contribute to this book and I'm thrilled to do so. Because of the nature of my testimony I will remain anonymous.

Look at your feet for a second. No one has feet like yours. Everyone is different. And your shoes, *has anyone walked in your shoes lately?* There was a time in my life that there was no one I could turn to here on this earth who was going to be walking in my shoes in the years to come.

I was fortunate to be raised in a Christian home. Our family was at church any time the doors were open. We were all involved in various ways over the years. I was led to the Lord when I was five-years-old by my Sunday School teacher. I graduated from a Christian school then went to Bible College. After college I returned home and married a young man from school.

We had an uneventful courtship and disagreed on very few things. My husband's family warned me that he had a bad temper but having never seen him angry, I found it hard to believe. The following year our first child was born. We were both young, naïve and very inexperienced. It wasn't long until the pressure of having a family began to take its toll. I soon saw what his family was talking about. He stopped going to church, which caused many arguments between us. And when he got angry he threw things, broke furniture or threw me against the wall.

The months turned into years and our second child was born. I felt so lonely during this time that I couldn't wait for the baby to be born. Stress over finances, battles over church, you name it - the arguments became more frequent and more violent. I was often interrogated after retuning home from church. The pressure of that each week wore me down and I often opted not to go at all. That was the first of many compromises.

The following years were a vicious cycle as the tension built, abuse occurred until the honeymoon phase where I would experience relief. Stress began again, the tension escalated, and we were back where we started. With each round of the cycle, the abusive behavior increased in intensity. I had less ability to receive the "nice behavior" in the honeymoon phase, because I feared the next round of harm without an opportunity to recover emotionally from the past abuse. I couldn't seem to do anything right. It broke my heart to hear my children cry out to their daddy to not hurt mommy. Children should not have to grow up in such an environment.

This vicious cycle continued for several years, but I never said a word to family or friends about what was going on. I sat in my church pew, and looked around at the families and wondered if anyone knew. *Could they tell? Did I cover it well?* Then I looked at the women and thought to myself, "*Does her husband hurt her? How about that one, he looks loving but is he at home?*"

During this time, I struggled with being faithful in my walk with the Lord. I gave into anything that would keep peace, another compromise. Amazingly, things seemed to lighten up. There was more time between incidents. I was relieved but couldn't help wondering when the other shoe would drop. During this time, our third child was born. Our family was complete. Although I knew things were still not right in the marriage, I did sense a softening. I asked my pastor, whom I counseled with on occasion, if God would use the birth of a baby to reach my husband's heart. He assured me that nothing is too hard for God. He gave me a verse, Jeremiah 29:11, "*For I know the thoughts that I think toward you, says the Lord, thoughts of peace, and not of evil, to give you a future and a hope.*" (NIV) Having been in church my whole life, I was surprised that I had never heard that verse before. I hung on to that verse with all my might. Only the Lord could have known how much that verse would mean to me in the years to come.

It was only a year after the baby was born that the other shoe dropped. Our happy little family was again on rocky ground. This time there was no stopping it. It became worse than ever. I compromised with one thing after another to keep peace, but it was never enough. Ultimately, I had no peace - not with myself and not with the Lord. I not only battled the outward challenges but also those within. I became extremely depressed. I functioned in a fog most of the time. I was an emotional wreck. I felt there was no way out. Divorce was not an option - but death was. I had decided that I would rather face God prematurely then to continue to live in this hell. I began to plan and prepare. I could feel myself sinking into a deeper darker hole. I had lost any hope of having a normal peaceful life. I wanted to die! After every confrontation I would beg God to let me die!

A relative that I spent a lot of time with soon picked up on the signs and shared her concerns with my parents. That evening my father called and begged for me to come home. I packed my children and went home to my parents for a few days. The kids were very confused and I was feeling pulled in every direction. My husband was begging me to come home, making promises and deals with me. I couldn't take the pressure and agreed to go back to my own home. As I packed my things, my father asked me to stay. I explained that I needed to go back. As I continued packing, I could hear him sobbing in the kitchen. It broke my heart that I had caused so much pain for my parents. Boy is that wrong thinking. I didn't cause them pain. My situation and the abuse I was living in caused them pain. Too often women in my situation assume the blame for the abuse. No one deserves to be hurt, *NO ONE!*

Victims of abuse often live in a state of fear, confusion, and overwhelming sadness. And that I did! I was in constant fear, confused as to what I should do or not do and had a never-ending sadness. I left the church I was attending. I wanted to make a fresh start. I thought if we could attend where no one knew us, my husband would join us again in church. I was desperate to make this work. The children and I started attending a fairly new church. Amazingly, he joined us a short time after. It was a small church. The people were wonderful and the teaching was great! I made myself at home and began to get involved where I could. We attended as a family. The plan had worked, or so I thought!

My relationship with my husband was still rocky at best. There were now other friendships that I had concerns about. But being very trusting and naïve, I refused to heed warnings. I convinced myself that if I was more submissive and a better wife, things would be okay. Besides, I didn't want to rock the boat!

I continued to grow in my walk with the Lord, thanks to the teaching at this church and the accountability they provided for me. I wrestled the scriptures searching for truth. My pastor's wife suggested I keep a prayer journal. I began to journal often and to pray the scriptures.

Journal entry:

MONDAY

"*Lord, teach me the timing and sequence You have set for my life so that I may dance to Your beat for me.*"

TUESDAY

"*But as for me, I trust in You, O Lord. I say You are my God. My times are in Your hand. Deliver me from the hand of my enemies and from those who persecute me.*" Psalm 31:14-15

THURSDAY

"*Lord soften his heart, make him tender toward me. Bring a new spirit in this home.*"

"*Bind mercy and truth around my neck so I will find favor and high esteem in the sight of God and man.*" Proverbs 3:3-4

FRIDAY

"*Father, this may not be the life You chose for me. But, I know You can make all things good in Your time. Give me grace Lord to carry on each day. I know its times like these I draw close to You. I know You have a plan for me. Amen.*"

I wrote nearly every day. Praises, struggles, verses that touched my heart. I began to counsel with my pastor and his wife. They prayed often with me, shared verses and encouraged me whenever they could.

The marriage did not improve. To be honest, it seemed the more I grew in my faith the worse it got. But I held on and continued to journal from my heart.

Journal entry:

SUNDAY

"*Father, I trust in You, I know You will care for my every need. I know You will not give me more then I can bear. Increase my faith Lord! Amen.*"

MONDAY
"Oh Lord, I need You, this is so hard. I can't do this alone!"

WEDNESDAY
"I blew it today Lord! Now what? Note to self: Read Galatians 5:22-25....again!"

I believe the Lord brought me to this church to strengthen my walk, grow me in my faith and to develop a support system for such a time as this. Because the rug to my little world was about to be pulled out from under me! I discovered my husband was having affairs!

Have you ever cried so deeply it made you sick? I did! The pain was incredible. I sobbed for hours! I asked myself over and over again, *"Why, why, what did I do to deserve this?"* My mother hugged me and whispered between her own sobs, *"I wish I knew what to do for you!"*

My parents didn't know what to do for me. I didn't know what to do for me! But that was okay, because it forced me to turn to my Heavenly Father. It caused me to trust Him. It eventually caused me to get to know myself and I learned to stand strong, over time. But at the moment I could barely function. I threw myself into the arms of Jesus and cried. I begged God to spare my marriage. The kids were so confused. *How do you explain this to your children?* The wound was so deep. It was as if it bled constantly. I couldn't seem to find a band-aid big enough.

Journal entry:
"Forgiveness, what does that look like? Lord, You are the healer of broken hearts, heal mine!"

The weeks turned into months and nothing changed. The pressure became too much and he moved out. I mourned as if someone had died. But at the same time, I felt a sense of relief from the stress, violence and constant turmoil. The children were devastated and confused. I had no idea how to comfort them. I was hurting so badly myself. My life was full of dysfunction. I began to write my pain, and struggle in the form of poetry.

Journal entry:

A LOVE LOST

A love lost in the waves of life
Can it be found?

Tossed about in the raging sea
My heart is bound

Sinking beneath the stormy swells
Could it ever be found?

Then washed ashore, battered and tore
Amidst the crashing sound.

Buried beneath the sands of time
Bruised and beaten, hopeless and resigned

Crying out – I want to be found

Then snatches away by an angry wave
This love is gone, for all it gave.

The next few months were a mirage of death threats, being stalked, break-ins, broken furniture and visits from the police at home and at work. I still made excuses for him, therefore protecting him. The police gave me information for the shelter for abused women anyway. I found myself right back where I started, a circle of violence that had no end. I often wonder if things would have been different had I pursued a PFA (Protection From Abuse) order. But the Lord never gave me peace to do that. I'm convinced He was protecting me from something far worse.

Although I was consistent in my walk with the Lord, I was still struggling with very low moments. I had times of near meltdowns and dysfunction and many times wished I could die. I felt broken and was searching for an identity. Years of negative input had stripped me of any sense of self-worth. Often, women like myself find themselves in relationships in which they are told they are not only "bad", but worthless, stupid, ugly, untrustworthy, crazy, and inadequate mothers and wives. They are often isolated and alienated from anything which could reinforce their self-worth, they come to measure their worth, and see themselves, in the eyes of their abusers. That was my life!

A friend approached me and said she was afraid for me, that I was dysfunctional and recommended I see a Christian counselor. She told me she would pick up the tab for the first two visits if I were willing to go. She handed me a phone number and then added, "*She's expecting your call.*"

This was the first of many people that the Lord placed in my life, again for such a time as this. There were individuals who provided a safe house for me, others who provided funds for the counselor and other needs. It was amazing how God provided for us during that time. I saw the counselor for over two years! She helped me understand many things. She helped me realize that it is not "normal" to want to die. I began a very long road to recovery from the abuse, post-traumatic stress syndrome, co-dependency and depression.

Although the healing process was long and painful, I was finally out of my fog and could think and see clearly. It had become very evident that there was no change in my husband and that the violent tendencies were still very real. The pastor of my church was so concerned about the violence and getting caught in the middle of it that he purchased life insurance for himself. But even with that, he actually participated in the cycle of abuse and reinforced the pattern with his insistence upon my spending time with my husband. He was constantly putting me in harms way. I met with him one afternoon. I reminded him of the many violent incidents and explained I was afraid he would get me killed. I asked him, "*Why? So you can say to God be the glory?*" He replied with a very bold, "*Yes!*" His response shocked me and convinced me I needed to find another church before his ignorance got me killed!

After seeking Biblical counsel, I filed for divorce. It was the only way to break free of the violent grip he had on me. Please understand that *I am not promoting divorce.* God hates divorce. He hates what it does to the lives of those involved. It's not what God intends for marriage and it's not a cure all for difficult marriages. To be perfectly honest, you just trade one set of problems for another. But, we were finally safe.

I was back to looking for another church and my search brought me to Christian Fellowship Church. I spoke with the pastor about my situation and he invited my children and me to come and let the church minister to us. Over the years, God has brought people in my life that have been a huge part of the healing process. It's difficult to summarize all that I've been through and all that the Lord has done for me. I've learned so much and have grown in many ways. I'm a very different person now. The woman who was battered no longer exists. The Lord has brought a new life to her body and that's who you see today.

There are many women who carry the same painful secret that I did for over 10 years. To tell or not to tell about abuse or violence is a dilemma. Each individual needs to assess his or her own situation and find ways to talk with minimal harm to him or herself.

According to Psalm 44:20-21, you can know that God knows the secrets of the heart. In Proverbs 25:9-10 it says that sharing the secret belongs to the person who has the secret. And in Matthew 18:15-29, sharing of the secret is needed for support and for dealing with the offender. But know that you are one of God's sheep, according to Psalm 23, to be cared for, to be protected, to celebrate with and to be comforted. Keep in mind, there is hope. There is always hope in the Lord, even in the worst of times.

All those years I kept coming back to the verse that my pastor gave me from Jeremiah. The Lord brought peace to my life and a loving godly man. Adam* was exactly what I needed in my life. We were married and began to blend a family together. No easy task with the road that my children and I had traveled. God has blessed me with a husband with the patience of Job and the wisdom of Solomon. He's more than just my husband; he is my best friend. I now believe there is such a thing as a soul mate!

These experiences that we have in our lives leave us feeling like we are alone, but we're not. We should be trusting in God in all things, being thankful and having gratitude to God for all things, even the shoes on our feet! I truly believe that! I've been given the opportunity to make a difference in someone's life because of what I've lived, someone who may be reading this very book. If I can reach out to just one person, it will make all that I've experienced worth it.

I promised the Lord that I would rise to the occasion, to share the beauty God has given me from the ashes of my life and share with you that He keeps His promises and will restore what the locust have eaten, just as He did for the children of Israel. If you are walking in my shoes, please get help! Contact your church, a shelter, friends or family. You do not have to live like this. *You can be safe! Will your story end like mine?* Maybe. Maybe not. But I assure you God has a plan for you written on His heart and it's full of *HOPE!*

I am thankful for my life circumstances. Although it was difficult, it has brought me to where I am today. I'm so thankful for life. I am so thankful that God is the healer of broken hearts!

Disclaimer:

The identity of the writer has been kept anonymous for her protection and the protection of her family. Domestic violence is real and dangerous. Although the writer is in a safe relationship today she still carries a justified fear of her abuser.

Chapter Seventeen:

A New Normal
By Mary Sensenig

"The greatest assets we leave behind are the ones
we leave behind."
-Mrs. Arlene Andrews

My story begins as an average child born into a Christian home that was stable and loving. It felt peaceful and full of love. Each summer I attended Good News Club (a ministry of Child Evangelism Fellowship) in our neighbor's backyard. At the age of 9, I realized I needed to ask Jesus into my heart. When the Good News Club teacher asked if anybody wanted to accept Jesus into his or her heart, I knew I wanted to. So, I met her after Club on the front porch and we prayed together. I knew then that the Holy Spirit was living in my heart. That experience I did so long ago becomes more real to me every day. But as I became a teenager, I wanted to do my own thing. However, I still knew Who was in control.

I met Floyd Sensenig when I was 15 years old, but I didn't date him until later. We were married in 1969. We had two boys, Brian Scott and Shawn Ryan. They were great boys, but we wanted to have one more. Along came a daughter, Amy Jo.

Amy came during a very stressful time in our family. When I was in my 7th month of pregnancy, Floyd was in a work accident and had to have his leg amputated. He was very sick with an infection during that time. By the grace of God, He spared Floyd's life so he was able to see our daughter being born.

Amy became Daddy's little girl – she stayed Daddy's little girl all through her life. She loved the things her dad loved and enjoyed being outside working side-by-side with him instead of inside cooking and cleaning with me.

We were an active family. We traveled, snowmobiled, motorcycled, went to the mountains, water skied, and did anything else that was adventurous.

Floyd showed our children that life didn't stop just because he lost his left leg. He was a very positive person. He had a very infectious personality. People gravitated to him. He loved people and was always willing to help where he could. Maybe it was the widowed lady next door or the neighborhood that needed snow removal or just someone who needed something fixed – Floyd quietly and faithfully served others.

On December 28, 2007, my world was turned upside down in an instant. I was at work (our family business – Sensenig & Weaver Well Drilling) finishing up year-end payroll when our rig operator

On a Snowmobiling Trip

Mary & Floyd in Alaska

Mary & Her Grandchildren

phoned. Our secretary, Kate, answered and the rig operator asked for me, which seemed rather unusual. I will never forget his words to me. He said, "*Floyd needs help.*"

My response to him was, "Is he living?"

He replied, "*He has a pulse.*" That told me a lot. He was barely living. Kate and I immediately began praying.

I called our children – as much as I could – and we rushed to Penn State Milton S. Hershey Medical Center. Amy and I traveled together. Our sons came as soon as they could. Driving to the hospital seemed to take extra long. I wanted to get there and yet I was scared to find out the truth.

Pastor Fred Raupp (one of our pastors at Christian Fellowship Church) was already at the hospital when Amy and I got there. We were supposed to wait in a room until the doctor came to give us an update, but I needed to know now. I looked at Pastor Fred and asked him, "Is Floyd gone?"

He reluctantly had to say, "Yes." I felt like I couldn't breathe. After that moment, life took on a whole new meaning for my family and me. There were emotions in me that I never knew existed.

The Sunday night after the accident I was sitting in bed

fearing that I would never get a good night's sleep again. As that fear was overwhelming me, I heard God say to me in the most loving voice, "*I will take care of you.*" I felt the softest arms lay my body down and I fell asleep. I never had trouble sleeping due to the accident ever since. His presence was so real to me that night.

Everything about my life changed. No more "husband and wife". The family unit changed. It became "Mother and children", "Grandmother and grandchildren." "Dad" and "Grandpa" are only a memory now. But, I do thank God for the memories!

As life continues, I am learning a lot about myself as a widow (I do not like that word, "widow"). I have felt the truth of God's promise about the "calm in the middle of the storm." Now that I live alone, I wake up talking to God. There are times when I feel His arms circled around me protecting me. My favorite Scripture through all of this has been Isaiah 41:10, "*So do not fear, for I am with you; do not be dismayed, for I am your God. I will strengthen you and help you; I will uphold you with My righteous right hand.*" At first I kept Floyd's Bible open on the dining room table with this verse highlighted so that every time I walked past his Bible, I would read it. What a blessing it was to have that promise to me.

The tragedy has opened my life to many "widow" friends. We all agree it's nice to have met each other, but we never asked to be in this group.

God is continually leading me in new paths - paths that I thought I would never go on – especially without Floyd. I - have been and am – very blessed to have my family, friends, co-workers, and my church family to support me every step of the way. As I adjust to this "new normal", I realize that I have to take many steps alone, but always with God's direction.

I have struggled with the fact that Floyd lost his life through an accident. There are those "what if only" times, but God says in Ecclesiastes 8:8, "*No man has power over the wind to contain it; so no one has power over the day of his death.*" Floyd's days were numbered and so I can't or couldn't have changed the day or hour.

In the year and a half that Floyd went Home to Heaven, I have experienced the death of my mother-in-law and my mother.

Mary, her parents & her son, Shawn & his family

The Sensenig Family

Our oldest son got married, I've had to care for my elderly father-in-law and father, our daughter, Amy, had her first child, I was in a car accident that involved a bicyclist (unfortunately, the girl never saw me stopped at a stop sign and ran into the back of my car), and I had to buy a new car. Some of these events were joyful, some were painful, but all were experienced without Floyd. I have learned from God, through Scripture, that *"the LORD will be your everlasting light, and your days of sorrow will end."* At times there are still many struggles with emotions of all kinds, but somehow God takes care of me and He will take care of you just as He promises!

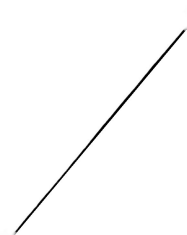

Chapter Eighteen:
Life Lessons
By Vivian Hertzler

"Come apart so you don't come apart!"
-Marian Horst

1. I am not an accident
- *"For you created my inmost being; You knit me together in my mother's womb."* Psalm 139:13
- *"Your eyes saw my unformed body. All the days ordained for me were written in your book before one of them came to be."* Psalm 139:16
- *"Praise be to the God and Father of our Lord Jesus Christ, who has blessed us in the heavenly realms with every spiritual blessing in Christ. For He chose us in Him before the creation of the world to be holy and blameless in His sight. In love He predestined us to be adopted as His sons through Jesus Christ, in accordance with His pleasure and will — to the praise of His glorious grace, which He has freely given us in the One He loves."* Ephesians 1:3-6

2. Where I had been in life is a part of God's plan for me
- *"Therefore, if anyone is in Christ, he is a new creation; the old has gone, the new has come!"* 2 Corinthians 5:17

3. God is in control of my circumstances and the people around me
- *"Though I walk in the midst of trouble, You preserve my life; You stretch out Your hand against the anger of my foe, with Your right hand You save me. The LORD will fulfill His purpose for me; Your love, O LORD, endures forever — do not abandon the works of Your hands."* Psalm 138:7,8
- *"You hem me in—behind and before; You have laid Your hand upon me."* Psalm 139:5

4. Anger at God and others must be faced and dealt with
- *"He is like a tree planted by streams of water, which yields its fruit in season and whose leaf does not wither. Whatever he does prospers."* Psalm 1:3
- *"'No longer will the people of Israel have malicious neighbors who are painful briers and sharp thorns. Then they will know that I am the Sovereign LORD.'"* Ezekiel 28:24
- *"If we confess our sins, He is faithful and just and will forgive us our sins and purify us from all unrighteousness."* 1 John 1:9

- *Forgiveness is surrendering my right to hurt someone because they hurt me.*

5. My purpose for being here is not be happy, but to make my Creator happy

- *"The LORD delights in those who fear Him, who put their hope in His unfailing love."* Psalm 147:11

6. Trusting God completely will bring me joy no matter what my circumstances may be

- *"Trust in the LORD with all your heart and lean not on your own understanding; in all your ways acknowledge Him, and He will make your paths straight."* Proverbs 3:5,6

7. Life under God's control will be an adventure no matter what my age

- *"Even to your old age and gray hairs I am He, I am He who will sustain you. I have made you and I will carry you; I will sustain you and I will rescue you."* Isaiah 46:4
- *"There was also a prophetess, Anna, the daughter of Phanuel, of the tribe of Asher. She was very old; she had lived with her husband seven years after her marriage, and then was a widow until she was eighty-four. She never left the temple but worshiped night and day, fasting and praying."* Luke 2:36,37 (Anna committed to fasting & praying)

8. My body is God's Temple – I must give it proper care

- *"Do you not know that your body is a temple of the Holy Spirit, who is in you, whom you have received from God? You are not your own; you were bought at a price. Therefore honor God with your body."* 1 Corinthians 6:19-20
- *"So whether you eat or drink or whatever you do, do it all for the glory of God."* 1 Corinthians 10:31
- *"Their destiny is destruction, their god is their stomach, and their glory is in their shame. Their mind is on earthly things."* Philippians 3:19

9. Enjoy what IS before IT isn't

- *"Why, you do not even know what will happen tomorrow. What is your life? You are a mist that appears for a little while and then vanishes."* James 4:14
- *"Be joyful always; pray continually."* 1 Thessalonians 5:16, 17 Give thanks in *all* circumstances.
- *"This is the day the LORD has made; let us rejoice and be glad in it."* Psalm 1189:24